INSPIRED!

A Drama with Music

by Lisa Soland

All Original
Play Publishing

INSPIRED: A DRAMA WITH MUSIC
Written by Lisa Soland
Copyright © 2023 by Lisa Soland

Published in 2024 by All Original Play Publishing
P.O. Box 32381
Knoxville, TN 37930
AllOriginalPlays@gmail.com

First Edition: April 2024
Printed in the United States of America
Graphic Design by All Original Play Publishing
Photography by Steven Wilson

ISBN: 978-1-956218-35-0
Library of Congress Control Number: 2024905426

What they're saying about...

INSPIRED!
A Drama With Music

"*Inspired!* is a testament to Soland's mastery of taking difficult historical material, drilling it down to the raw emotional truth, and humanizing it in play form. It is bold storytelling of extreme challenges of faith, renewed strength, and the creation of six now-familiar hymns. Soland's *Inspired!* makes it impossible to casually sing them ever again."

– Melanie Ewbank, Producer, Actress, and Playwright

"I was delighted to attend the first reading of Ms. Soland's new play *Inspired!* which was so very moving. If only there were a way the new play could be seen across the United States! The message will leave your spirit super-charged!"

– Donna Cielma, Executive Director at Christian Counseling Center of Cumberland County

"Lisa Soland has devoted her significant abilities to writing and sharing her new play *Inspired*! The inspirational stories of these seven hymn writers include John Newton, Louise Stead, and Martin Luther. All had deep personal faith and commitment to Jesus Christ."

– Sam Polson, Lead Pastor of West Park Baptist Church

"I loved *Inspired!* Playwright Lisa Soland has done an amazing job once again. She's captured the heart and soul of what these hymn writers were all about. Every scene is captivating and deeply moving. I couldn't put it down."

– Deborah York, Executive Director of the Sergeant York Patriotic Foundation and great-granddaughter of Alvin York

(The world-premiere cast of Inspired!: Jeannine
Brown, Christiane Frith, Joe Casterline, Lisa Soland,
Kris Phillips, and Max Horsewood.
Photo by Steven Wilson.)

*This play is dedicated to the original cast and crew
who helped actualize the vision.*

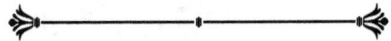

CAST of CHARACTERS

GUITARIST/SINGER: Can be either a guitarist or keyboardist who sings and writes Christian songs.

MARTIN LUTHER: Male, 40s or 50s.
SCHOOLTEACHER: Male, 40s or 50s.
HORATIO SPAFFORD: Male, 40s or 50s.
(These three roles can be played by the same actor.)

DEMONS 1 and 2: Two, male or female, any age.

JOHN NEWTON: Male in his 40s, 50s, or 60s.
(He can also play one of the two Monks.)

MAIN NARRATOR: Male or female, any age.
(MN can also play Demon 2.)

WARNER SISTERS NARRATOR: A woman, 30s.
ANNA SPAFFORD: A woman, 30s.
(These two roles can be played by the same woman. She can also play Demon 1.)

LONGFELLOW NARRATOR: Male or female, any age.

LOUISA M. R. STEAD: A woman in her 40s.
(She can also play one of the two Monks.)

PLACE & TIME

ACT ONE:
Scene 1: 1527
Scene 2: 1772
Scene 3: 1860
Scene 4: 1863

ACT TWO:
Scene 1: 1873
Scene 2: 1882, then modern day

INSPIRED! A DRAMA WITH MUSIC received its world premiere in the Hub at West Park in Knoxville, Tennessee, on November 9, 2023. It was directed by Lisa Soland, Max Horsewood was the musical director, Ben Davy was the technical director with Stefan Holt as his assistant, and Charlene Bledsoe was the costume director.

The show was subsequently produced at the Palace Theatre in Crossville, Tennessee, on November 28, 2023. The cast for both productions was as follows:

GUITARIST/SINGER .... Max Horsewood
MARTIN LUTHER/SCHOOLTEACHER/HORATIO SPAFFORD .... Joe Casterline
JOHN NEWTON .... Greg Helton
MAIN NARRATOR & DEMON 2 .... Kris Phillips
WARNER SISTERS NARRATOR, ANNA SPAFFORD, & DEMON 1 .... Christiane Frith
LONGFELLOW NARRATOR .... Lisa Soland
LOUISA M. R. STEAD .... Jeannine Brown

INSPIRED! was then produced for Knoxville Area Rescue Mission on April 13, 2024, with Pianist Taber Gable as Musician/Singer. Deborah York then produced the play at the Jamestown Community Center in Jamestown, Tennessee, on May 11, 2024. Both of these performances were to help provide meals, shelter, clothing, and care for those in need.

A staged reading of the play was presented in Knoxville, Tennessee, on July 25, 2023, directed by Lisa Soland. *Guitarist/Singer* was played by Max Horsewood, *Martin Luther/Schoolteacher/Horatio Spafford* by Coke Morgan, *John Newton* by Greg Helton, *Main Narrator* by Kris Phillips, *Louisa M. R. Stead* by Caitlin Rose, and *Anna Spafford/Longfellow Narrator* by Lisa Soland.

DESCRIPTION

Inspired! A Drama With Music
is a theatrical event that tells the true stories behind the
famous hymns we have all come to know and love.
Included are "Amazing Grace," "It is Well With My
Soul," and "A Mighty Fortress is Our God."

Inspired!
takes place in various locations at various times
throughout history.

It is a full-length play with an intermission.
The original production used four males
and three females.

- 4 m, 3 f -

INSPIRED!

A Drama with Music

ACT ONE

Scene 1
"A Mighty Fortress is Our God"
- 1527 -

SETTING: *An antique desk/table with two antique chairs has been placed downstage center. On top of the desk/table rests a new Bible, an old Bible, other books listed in full on the "Properties" list, a Civil War lantern, lit throughout the play, two quill feather pen sets, two Victorian fountain pens, and homemade tea-stained paper on which the historical hymns have been written. There is a large antique trunk stage right. Hanging upstage center above the desk/table is an oil on canvas painting, "Christ in the Storm on the Sea of Galilee" by Rembrandt. There is an antique chair far stage left, along with a small trunk and two guitars with their stands. PowerPoint screens are hanging above the stage, right and left, displaying images that help to tell the stories.*

AT RISE: MARTIN LUTHER *is lying prostrate on the floor, stage left. GUITARIST/SINGER is sitting on his antique chair far stage left with his guitar.*

(LIGHTS UP.)

LUTHER: O God, Almighty God everlasting! how dreadful is the world!
(HE comes up on his knees.)
Behold how its mouth opens to swallow me up, and how small is my faith in Thee! Oh, the weakness of the flesh and the power of Satan! If I am to depend upon any strength of this world, all is over. Sentence is gone forth. O thou, my God, help me against the wisdom of this world. My God, where art thou? Come! I pray thee, I am ready.
(The GUITARIST/SINGER plays a chord on the guitar three times, providing the MONKS with their starting notes. Each MONK also has a pitch pipe offstage.)

SONG: STAY WITH ME, (REMAIN HERE WITH ME)

TWO MONKS: *(The MONKS enter, each from behind two hanging flats of material, upstage right and left. THEY sing a chant in two parts.)*
STAY WITH ME. REMAIN HERE WITH ME, WATCHING AND PRAYING, WATCHING AND

PRAYING. STAY WITH ME. REMAIN HERE
WITH ME, WATCHING AND PRAYING,
WATCHING AND PRAYING.

(The MONKS stop singing and exit.)

LUTHER: *(HE rises and stands left of desk/table, then
delivers the famous closing lines of the speech
from the Diet of Worms.)*

"If my judgment is not in this way brought into
subjection to God's word, I neither can nor will
retract anything; for it cannot be either safe or
honest for a Christian to speak against his
conscience. Here I stand. I cannot do otherwise.
God help me. Amen."

*(To the audience, sarcastically regarding
himself.)*

Martin Luther—

[POWERPOINT image of Martin Luther.]

LUTHER: "Priest, Heretic, Outlaw." I did not see what I
did as an "act of heresy," but I suppose it was. I
did not intend to incite the Protestant
Reformation, though some say it was
unavoidable. I simply wanted to introduce, for
intellectual debate, rightful criticisms of The
Church as I could best state them. So, I
hammered my 95 Theses to the church door...

[POWERPOINT of the church.]

LUTHER: ...in Wittenberg, *(Pronounced Vittenberg.)* Germany, where I lived.

(Explaining to the audience.)

The Church believed that truth had been given, once and for all, to The Church, and The Church was to deliver that truth to believers. But God gave His Word, the Bible...

(Referring to the one on the desk/table.)

...to us all, not just The Church. We must completely rely on this...

(HE holds up the Bible.)

...as our source for our belief, not The Church.

(HE explains.)

According to The Church, in order to reduce my time in purgatory...

(LUTHER crosses stage right of desk/table.)

...I must buy an indulgence, a piece of paper, *from them.*

(Picks up paper from desk/table.)

That will get me into heaven faster. But I have read and re-read the New Testament, and the purchasing of indulgences has no impact whatsoever on whether or not people get into heaven. Our only way to obtain God's pardon for sin is this—

(HE holds up the Bible.)

—our faith in Jesus, and not good works.

(Returns Bible.)

So, as you can see, my ideas were in conflict with The Church, who wanted total control for, perhaps, the purposes of profit, dare I say. And there was The Church, or there was heresy. Eventually, I was summoned to appear before the Diet of Worms... *(Pronounced Vorms.)*

[POWERPOINT of the Imperial Free City of Worms, Germany.]

LUTHER: ...and the political authorities demanded that I recant my books, which had been copied and distributed. I was threatened with severe punishment, but I refused. I had to be convinced by Scripture, not by Popes and Councils who so often contradicted themselves, and I was not. I was not convinced. My conscience is captive to the Word of God, so help me.
(Beat.)
Those in charge then sought to kill me, but my defender, Prince Frederick...

[POWERPOINT image of Prince Frederick.]

LUTHER: ...hid me away at... *(Pronounced Vartburg.)* ...Wartburg Castle.

[POWERPOINT of Wartburg Castle.]

LUTHER: *(HE crosses to the left of desk/table and sits.)* It was there I translated the New Testament from Greek into the modern language of German...

[POWERPOINT of Luther's original Bible.]

LUTHER: ...a language that would be attainable to the masses. The people, themselves, would now understand that a pathway to heaven is not based on a person's good works here on earth, and The Church did not like that. And with the help of the printing press, this new Bible...
(HE lifts up the Bible.)
...*w*as published and distributed as well.
(Sarcastically.)
So, you can see why I was so popular.

[POWERPOINT goes to black.]

LUTHER: *(GUITARIST/SINGER quietly begins the instrumental of "A Mighty Fortress is Our God.")* During this difficult time of isolation in the castle, I also wrote some hymns. This one here...
(HE holds up the sheet music.)
...was thought of as my "Battle Hymn of the Reformation," but I did not write it to celebrate the Reformation. *My* working title was "A Hymn of Comfort" because "comfort" was in such high demand.
(GUITARIST/SINGER fades out the music. LUTHER rises.)
In August 1527, the bubonic plague fell upon Wittenberg. *(Pronounced Vittenberg.)* John, the Elector of Saxony, ordered me and my wife Katharina, who was pregnant, to leave town, but I refused.

(LUTHER crosses downstage center onto thrust.)

Instead, we turned our home into a hospital and watched many of our dearest friends die a quick and painful death. Fear is a tool of Satan's to defeat us. It hinders us from making wise decisions and causes us to lose hope, which destroys our faith. This is why God reminds us throughout scripture, over and over again, to 'fear not.'

(LUTHER crosses upstage right.)

When the plague was over, one-third of the population was dead. Then, a dear friend was burned at the stake, our son became ill, and in May of '28, our daughter Elisabeth died, following six months of a battle I had with God in prayer to save her!

(HE crosses to stage left of desk/table.)

I was exhausted, you see, and suffering from severe depression. Yet, throughout these horrific events, I chose to rely upon scripture. *(Lifts Bible.)* I found my comfort in the Psalms...

(HE opens the Bible.)

...and trusted in the unchanging promises of Jesus.

(HE pulls out his writing chair.)

It was during this time I wrote "A Mighty Fortress is Our God," based on Psalm 46.

(GUITARIST/SINGER plays the introduction of the song quietly while LUTHER sits and reads from the Bible.)

"Be still, and know that I am God. I will be exalted among the nations; I will be exalted in the earth!"
(LUTHER slowly picks up his feather pen and begins to write the hymn. GUITARIST/SINGER plucks chord three times.)

SONG: STAY WITH ME, (REMAIN HERE WITH ME)

TWO MONKS: *(Together, the MONKS step from behind their upstage curtains and sing this chant in two-part harmony.)*
STAY WITH ME. REMAIN HERE WITH ME, WATCHING AND PRAYING, WATCHING AND PRAYING.
(The MONKS repeat this chant until their exit toward the end of the scene.)

SONG: A MIGHTY FORTRESS IS OUR GOD

GUITARIST/SINGER: *(HE begins the song, timing it along with the chant.)*
A MIGHTY FORTRESS IS OUR GOD, A BULWARK NEVER FAILING; OUR HELPER HE, AMID THE FLOOD, OF MORTAL ILLS PREVAILING: FOR STILL OUR ANCIENT FOE, DOTH SEEK TO WORK US WOE; HIS CRAFT AND POWER ARE GREAT, AND, ARMED WITH CRUEL HATE, ON EARTH IS NOT HIS EQUAL.

DEMON 1: *(From her hiding position in the rolls of the curtain, upstage right.)*
　　The Christian shoemaker does his Christian duty not by putting little crosses on the shoes but by making *good* shoes. If you're going to write a hymn, Martin, it better be *good*. Can you write a *good* hymn, Martin?

LUTHER: *(Under his breath, to self.)*
　　He knows me by name.
　　(Throughout, LUTHER does his best to ignore the voices/demons.)
　　The song will celebrate the sovereign power of God over *everything*—good *and* evil—and the assurance we have in God because of His Son, Jesus.

DEMON 2: *(His voice comes from his hiding place in the large trunk, stage right.)*
　　If you want to change the world, Martin, you won't do it by writing a "hymn."
　　(DEMON 2 cracks open the lid.)
　　Another hymn about Him. I promise you, no one will care. Not really.

DEMON 1: *(Pokes head out.)* Haven't you done enough already?

DEMON 2: *(Steps out of trunk.)* What do you know of God?

LUTHER: Belief does not depend on what one *knows* about God but on a personal relationship *with* God, which is attainable through the sacrificial, *loving death* of Jesus Christ.
　　(The DEMONS make their way stage left.)

GUITARIST/SINGER: *(GUITARIST/SINGER sings acapella throughout.)*
DID WE IN OUR OWN STRENGTH CONFIDE, OUR STRIVING WOULD BE LOSING; WERE NOT THE RIGHT MAN ON OUR SIDE, THE MAN OF GOD'S OWN CHOOSING: DOST ASK WHO THAT MAY BE? *(DEMON 1 whispers in LUTHER'S ear.)* CHRIST JESUS, IT IS HE; LORD SAB-A-OTH, HIS NAME, FROM AGE TO AGE THE SAME, *(DEMON 2 whispers in LUTHER'S ear.)* AND HE MUST WIN THE BATTLE.

DEMON 1: *(The DEMONS cross each other upstage center. Then, DEMON 1 stations herself stage right, and DEMON 2 stage left.)*
You should have never deceived the Church, Martin. You chewed off your own foot when you crossed them.
(DEMON 2 mimes gnawing off his foot.)

LUTHER: I love Truth, and Truth is given to believers, not to any *church.* Truth is in the Word of God for all who *choose* to believe.

DEMON 2: "Choose to believe?" I thought God chose you, Martin.

LUTHER: So many voices running through my head. I can't hear the lyrics. I can't hear the words to write them.
(The DEMONS cross each other again, upstage of the desk, and now DEMON 1 is stage left of the desk; DEMON 2 is stage right.)

DEMON 1: Ah, tisk, tisk, tisk. What a shame, Martin.

DEMON 2: *(Evilly crossing to LUTHER.)*
      Shame, shame, shame.
      (LUTHER holds up his hand and stops DEMON
      2. LUTHER senses them physically in the room.)

LUTHER: Ah, my ol' ancient foe crawling around inside
      my mind once more.
      (HE sets the pen down.)
      But are you inside my head or... *(Rises.)* ...are you
      here, in this very room?

GUITARIST/SINGER: *(HE sings acapella while the*
      DEMONS continue their movement, crossing
      each other upstage of the desk and returning to
      the opposite sides of the stage. The two monks
      continue to sing the same chant throughout.)
      AND THOUGH THIS WORLD, WITH DEVILS
      FILLED, SHOULD THREATEN TO UNDO US,
      WE WILL NOT FEAR...

LUTHER: "Fear not!"

GUITARIST/SINGER: *(HE continues to sing.)* FOR
      GOD HAS WILLED HIS TRUTH TO TRIUMPH
      THROUGH US. THE PRINCE OF DARKNESS
      GRIM, WE TREMBLE NOT FOR HIM; HIS
      RAGE WE CAN ENDURE, FOR LO! HIS DOOM
      IS SURE; ONE LITTLE WORD SHALL FELL
      HIM.
      (The MONKS stop singing the chant and exit,
      leaving LUTHER alone with the DEMONS.)

DEMON 2: *(Looking at LUTHER'S sheet of paper,*
      stage right of the desk.)
      "One little word?" But you're having difficulty
      writing even one!

DEMON 1: *(Looking at LUTHER'S sheet of paper too.)* Not one word, Martin. Tisk, tisk, tisk.
(The two DEMONS cross upstage of the desk once more. DEMON 1 is now stage right, and DEMON 2 is stage left.)

LUTHER: You can't hide from me like you do so many others. I'm aware you exist, and I know right where you are. There and there!
(LUTHER points them out.)

DEMON 1: *(The attack increases.)* You call yourself a Christian?!

LUTHER: *(HE stands up to DEMON 1 by pointing her out.)*
Accuser!

DEMON 2: *(The attack increases.)* All those people are dead now because of you.

LUTHER: *(HE stands up to DEMON 2 by pointing at him.)*
Deceiver!

DEMON 1: All that reformed blood on *your* hands, Martin.
(DEMONS cross toward LUTHER, shaking the blood off their hands.)

LUTHER: *(HE crosses downstage of the desk/table, composes himself, and stands against them with the truth.)*
The only blood that concerns me is the blood of my Savior, Jesus Christ...
(DEMONS cringe at the name of Jesus and back away.)
...and the knowledge of Him crucified.

(The DEMONS cringe again, backing away.)
I shall worship the Lord my God and him only shall I serve!!!
(LUTHER throws the ink well into the curtain at the DEMON 1, stage right. The DEMONS scatter, and finally, there is silence. LUTHER quickly kneels and begins to pray.)
O God, Almighty God everlasting! Behold me prepared to lay down my life for thy truth, suffering like a lamb. And though the world should be thronged with devils, my soul belongs to thee and will abide with thee forever!
(LUTHER opens his eyes and rises while looking about the stage.)
I have driven the devil away with ink.
(Beat.)
Come, Lord Jesus! Your servant is waiting.
(MARTIN LUTHER quickly sits at the desk/ table, picks up his pen, and writes.)
GUITARIST/SINGER: *(GUITARIST/SINGER rises from the chair. HE sings acapella, raises the key of the song one step, and sings clearly and loudly.)*
THAT WORD ABOVE ALL EARTHLY POWERS, NO THANKS TO THEM, ABIDETH; THE SPIRIT AND THE GIFTS ARE OURS, THROUGH HIM WHO WITH US SIDE-ETH: LET GOODS AND KINDRED GO, THIS MORTAL LIFE ALSO; THE BODY THEY MAY KILL: GOD'S TRUTH ABIDETH STILL, HIS KINGDOM IS FOREVER.

LUTHER: *(HE sets his pen down on his desk and rises.)* The song is complete. God may do with it as He will. Amen.

(LIGHTS FADE to low.)

[POWERPOINT slide of the following words: Inscribed on the base of Luther's tomb are the words "A Mighty Fortress is Our God." It was written by the most influential figure of the Western world during the greatest period of German history and is thought to be the greatest hymn ever written."]

(POWERPOINT and LIGHTS OUT. LUTHER exits.)

End of Scene

ACT ONE

Scene 2
"Amazing Grace"
- 1772 -

(LIGHTS UP on JOHN NEWTON standing stage right of the desk/table. MAIN NARRATOR stands downstage center on thrust.)

JOHN NEWTON: I try to write a hymn a week to accompany my sermons and often call upon Luther's *Mighty Fortress* for inspiration. But sometimes, writing costs me so much thought and study that I hardly do anything else.

MAIN NARRATOR: It was late December 1772 in Olney, England, when a 47-year-old Pastor and former slave ship captain needed a song for his New Year's Day church service.

JOHN NEWTON: The title. Hmm. "Grace." No, not just *grace.* "*Amazing* Grace." Yes! *(Sits.)* Taking into consideration *my* life, that is more definitive. *(HE writes the title on paper, then sees the Bible and picks it up.)*

MAIN NARRATOR: The scripture verse had been chosen —1st Chronicles 17.

JOHN NEWTON: *(Reading from the Bible.)*
"Then King David went in and sat before the Lord and said, 'Who am I, O Lord God, and what is my house, that you have *brought me thus far?*'"

MAIN NARRATOR: But he needed a hymn to
accompany the verse.
(HE crosses upstairs to stage left of desk/table.)
JOHN NEWTON: When it comes to grace
softening the hardest of hearts, I know of no case
more extraordinary than my own.
(Beat.)
"Amazing Grace, how sweet the sound. Yes."
(HE writes.)

[POWERPOINT image of John Newton.]

MAIN NARRATOR: John Newton was born in London
on July 24, 1725. He was the son of a merchant
ship commander who sailed the Mediterranean
Sea. His Christian mother, Elizabeth, spent hours
with him each day, teaching him portions of
scripture, poems, and hymns.
JOHN NEWTON: *(Rises, crosses stage right, singing
acapella.)*
WHEN I SURVEY THE WONDROUS CROSS...
MAIN NARRATOR: Young John could recite every one
of Isaac Watts' 750 songs.
JOHN NEWTON: *(Singing acapella, HE crosses stage
left.)*
JOY TO THE WORLD, THE LORD HAS
COME.
MAIN NARRATOR: His mother would say to him,
"Son, I am praying that someday you will become
a minister of the Word of God."

JOHN NEWTON: *(HE crosses stage right, singing acapella, then stays.)*
O GOD, OUR HELP IN AGES PAST, OUR HOPE FOR YEARS TO COME...
MAIN NARRATOR: Two weeks before his *seventh* birthday, his mother died of tuberculosis.
JOHN NEWTON: *(Singing acapella, crosses to right of desk.)*
...OUR SHELTER FROM THE STORMY BLAST AND OUR ETERNAL HOME.
(Sits and writes.)

[POWERPOINT goes to black.]

MAIN NARRATOR: When John Sr. retired, John Jr. continued his work but only as a *common* seaman. He fell into terrible sin and was forced to enlist in the Navy as a *midshipman.* When he tried to desert, he was publicly flogged, then reduced again to the rank of a *common* seaman.
(Beat.)
Newton was so humiliated that he contemplated suicide but eventually recovered. He was transferred to the slave ship Pegasus, which carried goods to Africa and then traded those goods for slaves. But John continued to commit such horrific atrocities that the crew abandoned him on a small island off the coast of Sierra Leone, Africa. He was given to a Duchess, placed in chains, and abused along with her other slaves.

About a year later, he was rescued by a sea captain sent by his father.

(JOHN begins to drink out of the silver mug on table.)

MAIN NARRATOR: John then made his way back onto yet another trade ship and continued to live a life so morally wicked that even his rough shipmates found his actions appalling.

JOHN NEWTON: *(HE rises, now drunk, shouting at crew mates.)*

Get your hands off me, you no good son of a biscuit eater!!!

MAIN NARRATOR: Once, in a drunken rage, Newton fell overboard into the sea.

JOHN NEWTON: *(HE throws a punch, which causes him to stumble down the stairs, stage right—overboard. HE shouts and waves his arms.)*

Help! Help!

MAIN NARRATOR: To save him, his fellow crew members shot him with a harpoon!

(MAIN NARRATOR mimes the shooting.)

JOHN NEWTON: *(Mimes the harpoon hitting him in the right thigh and screams.)*

AHHHH-OHHHH!

MAIN NARRATOR: *(HE gathers the rope into his hands, pulling JOHN up onto stage right.)*

They pulled him back onboard the ship like a speared whale.

(HE crosses to JOHN'S right and pulls the harpoon out of his right thigh.)

JOHN NEWTON: *(Screams again.)* AHHH-OHHHH!

MAIN NARRATOR: From that day forward, John walked with a limp.

JOHN NEWTON: *(Lying on his side, stage right.)* Hopeless. Pathetic. Appalling. No, *wretched.* I lived a *wretched* life.

MAIN NARRATOR: Yeah, pretty much.

JOHN NEWTON: *(HE rises.)* But Jesus Christ came into the world to save sinners, of whom I am the worst.

(HE crosses to the desk, sits, then writes while speaking the lines.)

"He saved a wretch like me."

MAIN NARRATOR: *(Still standing stage right.)* On March 21, 1748, they were on the ship Greyhound and on their way home when, in the middle of the night, the 22-year-old was tossed awake by a violent storm.

(SOUND CUE: Violent storm.)

[POWERPOINT image of a ship of the day on the ocean during a violent storm.]

JOHN NEWTON: *(HE crosses downstage, onto thrust.)* Ah yes, my "great turning day." My "day of deliverance."

MAIN NARRATOR: His room was flooding with seawater, so John rushed to the deck...

(JOHN runs up the stairs stage right to MAIN NARRATOR, who now plays the captain. HE stops JOHN with upstage arm.)
...but the captain stopped him and sent him back to get a knife.
(JOHN runs back down onto thrust and pulls a knife out of his pocket.)
The man who took his place on deck was quickly washed overboard and never seen from again.

JOHN NEWTON: *(HE puts the knife back in his pocket.)* Providence amongst the chaos! But still, like any man, God had a purpose for me!
(JOHN crosses USL and grabs hold of the wheel.)

MAIN NARRATOR: He made it to the wheel of the ship, and while trying to steer, the great blasphemer, as he called himself, began to pray.

JOHN NEWTON: *(Praying.)* God, if thou wilt get me safely ashore, I will serve thee forever.

MAIN NARRATOR: *(Now one of the crew, HE crosses onto thrust and mimes tearing sheets and plugging holes.)*
The crew below worked tirelessly, plugging the holes with bedsheets and strips of clothing.

JOHN NEWTON: *(Still battling with the wheel.)* Mercy, dear Lord, in heaven. But what mercy can there be for me?

MAIN NARRATOR: When all seemed lost, and the ship was going to sink, John cried out to God—

JOHN NEWTON: *(Shouting out.)* LORD, I BEG YOU. HAVE MERCY ON US!!!

(The storm ceases, and there is silence.)

MAIN NARRATOR: The storm eventually ceased, and Newton thought about what he'd said. He believed God answered his prayers and saved him, so for the rest of his life, he observed that day...

NEWTON & MAIN NARRATOR: March 21st.

MAIN NARRATOR: ...as the day of his conversion.

JOHN NEWTON: How precious did that grace appear the hour I first believed.

MAIN NARRATOR: In 1754, when Captain Newton was 29...

(JOHN crosses to right of desk, while MAIN NARRATOR crosses USL.)

...he returned home from the sea to stay.

[POWERPOINT of Newton's home.]

JOHN NEWTON: *(HE sits and writes.)*

"'Tis grace hath brought me safe thus far, and grace will lead me home."

(HE sees his book on the table and picks it up.)

MAIN NARRATOR: The former slave ship captain not only renounced slavery but became a devoted abolitionist. He published a book...

[POWERPOINT of the cover of the book "Thoughts Upon The African Slave Trade."]

MAIN NARRATOR: *(Continuing.)* ...on his eyewitness accounts of the horrific conditions on slave ships and the brutal atrocities practiced on slaves.

JOHN NEWTON: *(Rises, crosses DSR onto thrust while reading from his book.)*
"The condition of the unhappy slaves is in a continual progress from bad to worse. Their case is truly pitiable, from the moment they are in a state of slavery, in their own country; but it may be deemed a state of ease and liberty, compared with their situation on board our ships."

MAIN NARRATOR: *(Crosses a bit downstage.)*
They called it "The Middle Passage," and it took them 80 days to cross the great Atlantic. Hundreds of human beings, stacked one on top of the other, like books upon a shelf.

JOHN NEWTON: I have known them so close that the shelf would not easily contain one more.

MAIN NARRATOR: For 80 days.
(Silence.)

[POWERPOINT of slaves packed together on the ship.]

JOHN NEWTON: *(HE continues to read.)*
"Yet, perhaps, they would wish to spend the remainder of their days on ship board, could they know, before-hand, the nature of the servitude which awaits them, on shore."

MAIN NARRATOR: *(HE crosses onto thrust, but still upstage of John.)*

But out of the 3.4 million Africans transported in British ships, 450,000 died onboard before ever getting off the boat. On the first page of his published book, Newton wrote…

[POWERPOINT of this first page of his published book.]

JOHN NEWTON: Matthew 7, verse 12: "All things whatsoever ye would that men should do to you, do ye even so to them: for this is the law and the prophets."

MAIN NARRATOR: *(HE crosses to the front of thrust, parallel to John.)*
Newton's detailed true account gave abolitionists, like his parliamentarian friend, William Wilberforce…

[POWERPOINT image of William Wilberforce.]

MAIN NARRATOR: …the evidence needed to change the minds of people *who simply had no clue.*

JOHN NEWTON: It was not easy to write with coolness about this slave business. And especially not easy for me, who was formerly so deeply engaged in it for more than 30 years.
(HE crosses to the right of desk/table.)

MAIN NARRATOR: John educated himself in Latin, Greek, and Hebrew. He made up his mind to become an evangelical minister for the Church of

England. How important are a mother's
prayers?!
(HE crosses upstage left of desk.)

JOHN NEWTON: I can still hear her gentle voice.
(As his mother.)
"John, I am praying that someday you will
become a minister of God's Word."
(JOHN sits.)

MAIN NARRATOR: Out of the 280 hymns written by
John, "Amazing Grace" is by far the most
beloved.

JOHN NEWTON: The song is a testimony for what God
did for my life.

MAIN NARRATOR: All of those deeply imbedded
memories prepared John to write a song so
powerful, so anointed that it changed the lives of
countless people throughout the ages.

JOHN NEWTON: *(Spoken while writing.)* "But God,
who called me here below, will be forever mine."
*(MAIN NARRATOR crosses to the downstage
left very corner of the stage, while JOHN crosses
to the podium, located in the downstage right
very corner of the stage.)*

MAIN NARRATOR: His song "Amazing Grace" was sung
before Martin Luther King Jr. delivered his most
famous speech—

*[POWERPOINT of Martin Luther King Jr.
during speech.]*

NEWTON as MARTIN LUTHER KING JR.: *(Imitating Martin Luther King Jr.)*
"I have a dream that one day this nation will rise up and live out the true meaning of its creed. We hold these truths to be self-evident that all men are created equal."

MAIN NARRATOR: In South Africa when Nelson Mandela was released from serving 27 years in prison.

[POWERPOINT of Nelson Mandela during speech.]

NEWTON as NELSON MANDELA: *(Imitating Nelson Mandela.)*
"I stand here before you not as a prophet but as a humble servant of you, the people. Your tireless and heroic sacrifices have made it possible for me to be here today. I, therefore, place the remaining years of my life in your hands."

MAIN NARRATOR: In Germany, when the Berlin Wall fell to the ground.

[POWERPOINT of Reagan during speech.]

NEWTON as RONALD REAGAN: *(Imitating Ronald Reagan.)*
"Mr. Gorbachev, *(Beat.)* tear down this wall!!!"

MAIN NARRATOR: And it was sung to comfort a mourning nation following the attacks of 9/11.

[POWERPOINT of Bush with a bullhorn at Ground Zero.]

NEWTON as GEORGE W. BUSH: *(HE picks up a bullhorn masked beneath the podium and delivers the speech with it, imitating George Bush at Ground Zero.)*
"Terrorist attacks can shake the foundations of our biggest buildings, but they cannot touch the foundation of America. These acts shattered steel, but they cannot dent the steel of American resolve."

[POWERPOINT goes to black.]

(BOTH the MAIN NARRATOR and a now-aging JOHN cross in a few steps, stopping at the same time.)
MAIN NARRATOR: On December 21, 1807, with ill health and failing eyesight, Newton died nine months after witnessing the successful passage of the act for the abolition of slavery in Britain.
JOHN NEWTON: *(Spoken.)* "I once was lost but now am found, was blind but now I see."
MAIN NARRATOR: His gravestone reads:

[POWERPOINT of NEWTON's gravestone.]

SONG: AMAZING GRACE

(GUITARIST/SINGER begins to play the instrumental introduction to "Amazing Grace," while JOHN crosses downstage onto right side of thrust.)

MAIN NARRATOR: *(HE continues.)* "John Newton, clerk, once an infidel and libertine, a servant of slaves in Africa, was by the rich mercy of our Lord and Savior Jesus Christ, preserved, restored, pardoned, and appointed to preach the faith he had long labored to destroy."

JOHN NEWTON: *(JOHN sings verse 1, downstage right on thrust. In the Key of E.)*
AMAZING GRACE HOW SWEET THE SOUND, THAT SAVED A WRETCH LIKE ME. I ONCE WAS LOST, BUT NOW I'M FOUND, WAS BLIND, BUT NOW I SEE.
(MAIN NARRATOR crosses to an elderly JOHN and helps him cross up the stairs and back into his chair, stage right of the desk, while GUITARIST/SINGER sings.)

GUITARIST/SINGER: *(Sings verse 2.)*
'TWAS GRACE THAT TAUGHT MY HEART TO FEAR, AND GRACE MY FEARS RELIEVED. HOW PRECIOUS DID THAT GRACE APPEAR, THE HOUR I FIRST BELIEVED.
(GUITARIST/SINGER plays instrumental while JOHN speaks the following line, with MAIN NARRATOR standing to JOHN'S right for support.)

JOHN NEWTON: *(Spoken.)* My memory is nearly gone, but I remember two things: that I am a great sinner—and that Christ is a great Savior!
(JOHN sings verse 3 while GUITARIST/SINGER continues to play.)
THE LORD HAS PROMISED GOOD TO ME, HIS WORD MY HOPE SECURES. HE WILL MY SHIELD AND PORTION BE, AS LONG AS LIFE ENDURES.

NEWTON, MAIN NARRATOR, GUITARIST/SINGER:
(For verse 4, the GUITARIST/SINGER rises, the MAIN NARRATOR crosses stage right, and NEWTON remains sitting right of the desk/table. MAIN NARRATOR and NEWTON sing melody, and GUITARIST/SINGER sings harmony.)
THE EARTH SHALL SOON DISSOLVE LIKE SNOW, THE SUN FORBEAR TO SHINE. BUT GOD, WHO CALLED ME HERE BELOW, WILL BE FOREVER MINE.
(NEWTON rises and lifts hands to the Lord.)
YOU ARE FOREVER MINE.

[POWERPOINT goes to black.]

(LIGHTS fade. NEWTON and MAIN NARRATOR exit.)

End of Scene

ACT ONE

Scene 3
"Jesus Loves Me"
- 1860 -

(LIGHTS UP on WARNER SISTERS NARRATOR standing stage left.)

WARNER SISTERS NARRATOR: When life is difficult, it's hard to imagine that there might be *a purpose* for that difficulty. But in Christ, all things work together for good. There is *goodness* in that hardship; we just can't see it when we're in it.
(SHE crosses to downstage center and really asks the audience...)
Do any of you remember the first Christian hymn you learned? What was it?
(SHE acknowledges a couple of the responses by repeating them as they are shared but quickly moves on.)
Let me tell you a story about two sisters...
(SHE crosses stage right.)

[POWERPOINT of Susan and Anna Warner.]

WARNER SISTERS NARRATOR: *(SHE acknowledges the image on Powerpoint.)* ...Susan and Anna Warner. Their father was a New York City lawyer, and they were wealthy. But when they were both very young, their mother died, and in the "Panic of 1837" their father lost everything. They were forced to leave their mansion and move into an old Revolutionary War-era farmhouse on Constitution Island in the Hudson River opposite West Point.

[POWERPOINT of the Warner Sisters' home on Constitution Island.]

WARNER SISTERS NARRATOR: *(SHE continues.)*
The girls became devout Christians, but that did not change the fact that they barely had enough money to survive. *(Beat.)* In 1849, they realized their situation was not going to improve, so they decided to get to work.
(SHE crosses to left of desk/table and sits.)
They began to write, and they wrote and they wrote. The older sister, Susan...

[POWERPOINT of Susan Warner.]

WARNER SISTERS NARRATOR: *(SHE continues.)*
...became the first American author to sell over one million books. One of her 30 novels, written in 1860, was titled *Say and Seal.*
(SHE selects the actual heavy book from the desk/table, then rises.)
In Volume Two, there is a poem that was shared by the protagonist of the story...

(SCHOOLTEACHER enters from upstage left.)
WARNER SISTERS NARRATOR: *(Continues.)*
...a schoolteacher. One of his young students was dying...
(SCHOOLTEACHER and WARNER SISTERS NARRATOR sit downstage, slightly left. HE holds her in his arms; SHE holds the book. GUITARIST/SINGER plays softly the introduction to "Jesus Loves Me.")
...and the schoolteacher held the boy in his arms and read the four stanzas to him.
SCHOOLTEACHER: *(Spoken, not sung along with the guitar instrumental.)*
"Jesus loves me! This I know, for the Bible tells me so. Little ones to Him belong; they are weak, but He is strong."
(SCHOOLTEACHER and WARNER SISTERS NARRATOR rise.)
WARNER SISTERS NARRATOR: About two years later, William Bradbury...

[POWERPOINT image of William Bradbury.]

WARNER SISTERS NARRATOR: ...a musician and songwriter was reading Susan's book and was so inspired by this poem that he quickly put music to the words and added a chorus.
(GUITARIST/SINGER plays "Yes, Jesus Loves Me," the chorus. WARNER SISTERS NARRATOR sets the book on the desk.)

The simple tune quickly became one of the most popular Christian hymns of all time, but the song was especially loved by children.

SCHOOLTEACHER: *(To audience.)* Jesus said, "Unless we turn and become like children, we will never enter the kingdom of heaven."

(WARNER SISTERS NARRATOR crosses downstage onto thrust while SCHOOLTEACHER crosses stage right.)

WARNER SISTERS NARRATOR: Do you recognize this tune?

(SHE encourages the audience to raise their hands.)

I'll skip the first verse everyone knows and sing the other three verses for you as they were originally written in 1860. Please join us with the chorus.

(GUITARIST/SINGER rises.)

SONG: JESUS LOVES ME

WARNER SISTERS NARRATOR: *(Sings.)*
JESUS LOVES ME—HE WHO DIED
HEAVEN'S GATE TO OPEN WIDE;
HE WILL WASH AWAY MY SIN,
LET HIS LITTLE CHILD COME IN.

[POWERPOINT of the words to the chorus.]

ALL THREE: *(Singing.)*
> YES, JESUS LOVES ME, YES, JESUS LOVES
> ME, YES, JESUS LOVES ME—THE BIBLE
> TELLS ME SO!

> *[POWERPOINT screen goes to black.]*

WARNER SISTERS NARRATOR: *(Sings.)*
> JESUS LOVES ME—LOVES ME STILL,
> THOUGH I'M VERY WEAK AND ILL;
> FROM HIS SHINING THRONE ON HIGH,
> COMES TO WATCH ME WHERE I LIE.

> *[POWERPOINT of the words to the chorus.]*

ALL THREE: *(Sings.)*
> YES, JESUS LOVES ME, YES, JESUS LOVES
> ME, YES, JESUS LOVES ME—THE BIBLE
> TELLS ME SO!

> *[POWERPOINT screen goes to black.]*

WARNER SISTERS NARRATOR: *(Sings.)*
> JESUS LOVES ME—HE WILL STAY
> CLOSE BESIDE ME ALL THE WAY.
> THEN HIS LITTLE CHILD WILL TAKE
> UP TO HEAVEN FOR HIS DEAR SAKE.

> *[POWERPOINT of the words to the chorus.]*

ALL THREE: *(Sings.)*

> YES, JESUS LOVES ME, YES, JESUS LOVES
> ME, YES, JESUS LOVES ME—THE BIBLE
> TELLS ME SO! THE BIBLE TELLS ME SO!
> *(SCHOOLTEACHER exits upstage left.*
> *GUITARIST/SINGER sits in chair stage left.)*

WARNER SISTERS NARRATOR: Susan and Anna had
> no idea what would become of that little poem in
> her book. They simply found a skill they enjoyed
> and were good at—writing—and they wrote and
> they wrote, and they wrote. Then, they trusted
> God to take care of the rest.
> *(SHE turns to begin her exit upstage left, then*
> *turns back to the audience.)*
> Oh, by the way, the two Warner sisters also
> started a Sunday school on the island for the
> young men studying at West Point. On Sunday
> afternoons, the cadets would row over to the
> island...
> *(SHE crosses downstage center, rowing*
> *backward like on a boat.)*
>
> *[POWERPOINT of the island from the viewpoint*
> *of West Point.]*

WARNER SISTERS NARRATOR: *(Continues.)*
> ...and the sisters would serve them *lemonade and*
> *ginger cookies* while teaching them hymns and
> scripture. Every single one of those young men
> learned *"Jesus Loves Me"* from the women who
> wrote it. Susan died in 1885, and Anna in 1915...

(SHE crosses stage right.)
...but in that last year's group of Sunday school students from West Point, one of Anna's pupils was General Dwight D. Eisenhower...

[POWERPOINT of Eisenhower as a West Point cadet.]

WARNER SISTERS NARRATOR: *(Continues.)*
...the 34th President of the United States...

[POWERPOINT of Eisenhower as President.]

WARNER SISTERS NARRATOR: *(Continues.)*
...who obtained a truce in Korea and worked tirelessly during his two terms to ease the tensions of the Cold War.
(Crosses to center.)
Only two civilian women were buried in the cemetery at the U.S. Military Academy at *West Point*—and those women were Susan and Anna Warner.

[POWERPOINT of their gravestones at West Point, then POWERPOINT goes to black.]

(LIGHTS FADE as WSN exits USL.)

End of Scene

ACT I

Scene 4
"I Heard the Bells on Christmas Day"
- 1863 -

(LIGHTS UP on LONGFELLOW NARRATOR standing stage right of desk/table.)

[POWERPOINT image of a young Longfellow.]

LONGFELLOW NARRATOR: Henry Wadsworth Longfellow was the most famous American poet and writer of the 19th century. As a child, I remember his poem—Paul Revere's Ride.
(SHE picks up the lantern from the table and uses it as Paul Revere.)
"Listen, my children, and you shall hear of the midnight ride of Paul Revere. One if by land, and two if by sea; And I on the opposite shore will be."
(SHE returns the lantern to the table, then encourages audience participation.)
Raise your hand if you recognize these adages of his, still in use today—"Ships that pass in the night.
(Raises her hand to encourage and acknowledge those in the audience with their hands raised.)
"The patter of little feet."
(Raises her hand.)
"Into each life, some rain must fall."

(Raises her hand.)
Longfellow wrote poems about history, mythology, and legend, but only one poem about love—a sonnet, "The Evening Star."
(SHE gets down onto one knee.)
"O my beloved, my sweet Hesperus! My morning and my evening star of love!"
(Rises.)
He's writing of his intense love for a beautiful young artist by the name of Fanny Appleton. After seven long years of courting her, she finally agreed to marry Longfellow.

[POWERPOINT image of his wife, Fanny.]

LONGFELLOW NARRATOR: Blessed with five children, they made a beautiful life for themselves in Cambridge, Massachusetts, and became a national symbol of domestic love. But as Henry wrote, "Into each life, some rain must fall."
(SHE picks up the fan from the desk/table, then crosses onto thrust, downstage center.)
It was the summer of 1861, and the Longfellows were suffering through an unbearable heat wave. On July 9, Fanny wrote in her journal...
(SHE opens the fan and uses it to fan herself.)
"We are all sighing for the good sea breeze instead of this stifling land one, filled with dust. Poor Allegra is very droopy with heat, and Edie has to get her hair in a net to free her neck from the weight."

[POWERPOINT goes to black.]

LONGFELLOW NARRATOR: *(SHE uses the fan as scissors.)*
The next day, Fanny trimmed some of her daughter's heavy locks of hair. Wanting to preserve them, she placed them into an envelope and melted wax to seal the envelope shut. But something fell onto her lap, unnoticed. Then, that long-awaited summer breeze blew through the window and set her thin dress on fire. Fanny was instantly wrapped in flames.
(Crosses upstage left.)
To protect her children, she fled to Henry's study, and he tried frantically to extinguish the flames with a small rug, but to no avail. In complete desperation, he threw his arms around her, using his body to smother the fire, which severely burned his face, arms, and hands.
(Beat.)
Fanny suffered through the night then died the following morning. Henry could not attend her funeral. He had severe injuries of his own, and his soul was devastated. She was the love of his life, and now she was gone.
(Crosses to left of desk/table, sets down fan.)
A year after the incident, Longfellow wrote, "I can make no record of these days. Better leave them wrapped in silence. Perhaps someday God will give me peace." But tragedy was not finished with this family.

(GUITARIST/SINGER begins to play quietly on guitar, "Mine eyes have seen the glory of the coming of the Lord. He is trampling out the vintage where the grapes of wrath are stored. He have loosed the fateful lightning of His terrible swift sword. His truth is marching on.")

LONGFELLOW NARRATOR: *(SHE crosses stage right.)* In 1863, despite his father's disapproval, Longfellow's eldest son, Charley, ran off to fight in the Civil War.

[POWERPOINT of Charley Longfellow.]

LONGFELLOW NARRATOR: That December, Longfellow received word that Charles, now a lieutenant in the Army...
(SHE salutes.)
...had been severely wounded. A bullet passed under his shoulder blades, and it was thought that he would be paralyzed for life.
(GUITARIST/SINGER stops playing.
LONGFELLOW NARRATOR crosses to stage right of the desk/table.)
That Christmas, Longfellow's journal page remained empty. His grief finally silenced him, and he wrote no more.
(LONGFELLOW NARRATOR crosses to center stage, downstage of desk.)
The following year...

[POWERPOINT of Abraham Lincoln.]

LONGFELLOW NARRATOR: *(Continuing.)* ...Abraham
Lincoln was re-elected, and there was hope that
the war might soon come to an end. It was
Christmas Day, and Longfellow was lost in
thought when suddenly he heard the ringing of
the town's Christmas bells.
*(GUITARIST/SINGER begins to softly play the
introduction to the next song.)*
He listened intently and came to realize that no
matter what happens to us in this life, there
remains—steadfast and true—an eternal hope
that overcomes the heartbreaks we suffer here on
earth.
(SHE crosses to left of desk/table.)
Longfellow sat down and wrote the words to this
song.

[POWERPOINT goes to black.]

SONG: I HEARD THE BELLS ON
CHRISTMAS DAY

GUITARIST/SINGER: *(For verse 1, GS sings the melody
by himself as LN crosses to him. SHE sits on
small trunk and joins in with her guitar, with
Capo on 4, for verse 2.)*
I [C] HEARD THE BELLS ON [Dm]
CHRISTMAS DAY. THEIR [C] OLD FAMILIAR
[Dm] CAROLS [G7] PLAY.

AND [C] MILD AND SWEET THE [E] WORDS
[Am] REPEAT, OF [C] PEACE ON EARTH
GOOD [G7] WILL TO [C] MEN.

BOTH: *(For verse 2, BOTH sing melody.)*
I [C] THOUGHT / HOW, AS / THE [Dm] DAY
HAD COME, THE [C] BELFRIES OF ALL [Dm]
CHRIS-EN- [G7] DOM.
HAD [C] ROLLED ALONG THE 'UN [E]
BROKEN [AM] SONG, OF [C] PEACE ON
EARTH, GOOD [G7] WILL TO [C] MEN.

BOTH: *(Verse 3, GUITARIST/SINGER sings the
melody, LONGFELLOW NARRATOR sings
harmony.)*
AND [C] IN DESPAIR I [DM] BOWED MY
HEAD: "THERE [C] IS NO PEACE ON [DM]
EARTH," I [G7] SAID, *(Hold for 8.)*
"FOR [C] HATE IS STRONG AND [E] MOCKS
THE [Am] SONG (HOLD FOR 4) OF [C] PEACE
ON EARTH, GOOD [G7] WILL TO [C] MEN."
*(LONGFELLOW NARRATOR quickly moves her
Capo up to the 6th fret, raising the key. For
verse 4, SHE sings the melody, and GS sings the
harmony.)*
THEN [C] PEALED THE BELLS MORE [DM]
LOUD AND DEEP: "GOD [C] IS NOT DEAD,
NOR [Dm] DOTH HE [G7] SLEEP; *(Hold for 8.)*
THE [C] WRONG SHALL FAIL, THE [E] RIGHT
[AM] PREVAIL... *(Hold for 8.)*

LONGFELLOW NARRATOR: WITH [C] PEACE ON
EARTH...

GUITARIST/SINGER: *(Echoing.)* WITH PEACE ON
      EARTH.

LONGFELLOW NARRATOR: WITH [D] PEACE ON
      EARTH...

GUITARIST/SINGER: *(Echoing.)* WITH PEACE ON
      EARTH.

LONGFELLOW NARRATOR and GUITARIST/SINGER:
      WITH [C] PEACE—ON—EARTH—GOOD [G]
      WILL *(Hold for 2.)* TO [C] MEN." *(Hold for 8.)*

      *[POWERPOINT of an old Longfellow with his
      famous beard.]*

LONGFELLOW NARRATOR: *(SHE takes off the guitar
      and sets it on the stand.)*
      The peace that Longfellow referred to in the song
      he quoted from the Bible: Luke, Chapter 2, verse
      14: "Glory to God in the highest, and on earth
      peace, good will toward men."
      (SHE refers to the PowerPoint image.)
      That image became Longfellow's iconic look.

      *[POWERPOINT of the Longfellow postage
      stamp.]*

LONGFELLOW NARRATOR: *(Continues.)* Award
      medals, postage stamps, and countless
      photographs portrayed Longfellow with that
      beard, grown to hide the scars caused by that
      terrible fire.

[POWERPOINT goes to black.]

LONFELLOW NARRATOR: Jesus has scars, too.
(SHE points to the palms of her hands.)
Here and here. He got them when he willingly hung on the cross, putting out the flames of our sins forever. Without a second thought, Jesus threw himself over me and you so that now, when God looks down on us, He sees Jesus' beauty looking up at Him.
(Beat.)
Aren't you glad "God is not dead?" Aren't you glad "God does not sleep?" Patience. Trust in the Lord.
(SHE crosses onto thrust downstage center.)
"The wrong shall fail; the right prevails." In other words, the right will "prove more powerful than all opposing forces."
(Beat.)
We might not have peace on this earth right now. In fact, things may be looking mighty grim. In the midst of suffering, Longfellow wrote to a friend: "I do not believe anyone can be perfectly well, who has a brain and a heart." But, we can have "the peace which surpasses all understanding" when we trust our lives to the One who created us. His peace will sustain us. He will guide us through. Write these verses down; keep them with you, always—Romans 8:35-39.
(From memory.)

Apostle Paul wrote, "Who shall separate us from the love of Christ? Shall tribulation, or distress, or persecution, or famine, or nakedness, or danger, or sword? As it is written, 'For your sake we are being killed all the day long; we are regarded as sheep to be slaughtered.' No, in all these things we are more than conquerors through him who loved us."

(GUITARIST/SINGER starts playing quietly on guitar, "Mine eyes have seen the glory of the coming of the Lord. He is trampling out the vintage where the grapes of wrath are stored. He have loosed the fateful lightening of His terrible swift sword. His truth is marching on." Then fades out.)

LONGFELLOW NARRATOR: For I am sure that neither death nor life...

(WARNER SISTERS NARRATOR enters from USL and stands stage right.)

...nor angels nor rulers...

(JOHN NEWTON enters from USL and stands stage left of WARNER SISTERS NARRATOR.)

... nor things present nor things to come...

(MARTIN LUTHER enters from USL and stands stage left.)

...nor powers, nor height nor depth nor anything else in all creation, will be able to separate us from the love of God in Christ Jesus our Lord."

(GUITARIST/SINGER finishes "Glory Glory..." with a chord, helping LONGFELLOW NARRATOR find her first note.)

LONGFELLOW NARRATOR: *(Still standing DSC.)*
"THE WRONG SHALL FAIL, THE RIGHT PREVAIL..."
LONGFELLOW NARRATOR and WARNER SISTERS
NARRATOR: *(The two start on LN's ending note. LN crosses upstage and stands between NEWTON and LUTHER.)*
"JESUS LOVES ME, THIS I KNOW!"
LONFFELLOW NARRATOR, WARNER SISTERS
NARRATOR, and JOHN NEWTON: *(The three start on WSN's last note.)*
"I ONCE WAS LOST BUT NOW AM FOUND."
(THEY go up at the end.)
LONFFELLOW NARRATOR, WARNER SISTERS
NARRATOR, JOHN NEWTON, and MARTIN LUTHER:
(The four start on JOHN NEWTON'S last note that went up.)
"A MIGHTY FORTRESS IS OUR GOD!"
(THEY hold the note, then stop singing as the LIGHTS fade out. EVERYONE exits.)

[POWERPOINT photo of Warner Sisters that reads, "Please join us for THE WARNER SISTERS 'Lemonade and Ginger Cookies' in the lobby."]

End of Act One

ACT TWO

Scene 1
"It is Well With My Soul"
- 1873 -

(LIGHTS UP on MAIN NARRATOR standing on the thrust, downstage center.)

MAIN NARRATOR: In early 1871, Horatio Spafford...

[POWERPOINT of Horatio Spafford.]

MAIN NARRATOR: *(Continuing.)* ...a successful lawyer and committed Christian was living what we might call a "blessed" life. The Civil War was over, and the United States was experiencing an exploding economy. Spafford had been purchasing real estate in Chicago, where he lived with his wife Anna...

[POWERPOINT of Anna Spafford.]

MAIN NARRATOR: *(Continuing.)* ...and their four young daughters. On October 8, the Great Chicago fire broke out and destroyed all of Horatio's real estate investments. The family lost everything.

[POWERPOINT image of the Chicago Fire.]

MAIN NARRATOR: But the Spaffords were Christians
    and relied on their faith. They were personal
    friends with Dwight L. Moody…

[POWERPOINT of Dwight L. Moody.]

MAIN NARRATOR: … the famous evangelist of the day
    and had supported many of his crusades. For the
    next two years, Horatio and Anna devoted their
    time to helping the refugees of the fire.
    (MAIN NARRATOR crosses far stage right.)
    In 1873, the Spafford family purchased six
    tickets…
    *(HORATIO, wearing an overcoat and top hat,
    and ANNA, wearing a fashionable hat, shawl,
    and gloves, enter from upstage right and say
    goodbye there.)*
    …to board the Ville Du Havre and sail to
    Jerusalem, the Holy Land, to help Moody with
    his new evangelical campaign, "sharing the love
    of Christ with unbelievers."
    *(ANNA crosses stage left, both still waving
    goodbye.)*
    Just before sailing, Horatio was called to handle
    an urgent business matter.
    (HORATIO exits upstage right.)
ANNA SPAFFORD: On November 23, at 2 o'clock in the
    morning, halfway across the Atlantic Ocean, our
    luxury steamship collided with a British vessel…

[POWERPOINT image of two ships colliding.]

ANNA SPAFFORD: ...both moving at full speed. With the storm at its worst, we all rushed on deck and watched helplessly as the rising water quickly filled the boat. Our daughter, Maggie, who had been screaming since the crash, suddenly stopped and said with assurance, "God will take care of us, Momma." I remember Annie calling out, "Don't be afraid. The sea is His, and He made it." Then we watched the ship break in two, and when it collapsed into the ocean, the force pulled most of those floating on the surface down into the depths of the freezing water. I, too, was thrown into the sea with my baby daughter Tanetta in my arms, but the rough waves had their way with her. Within 12 minutes, 226 lives were lost, including our four daughters.

[POWERPOINT of the four daughters.]

ANNA SPAFFORD: I was found floating on a piece of wood, unconscious, and when I learned that all of our children were dead, I had to be physically restrained. "I want to die," I screamed. "I want to follow my dear ones! I cannot live without them!" But God told me, in a still, small voice: "You are spared for a purpose. You have work to do." God gave me four daughters; then, they were taken away. One day, I shall understand why. One day.

MAIN NARRATOR: In Chicago, her husband woke to the newspaper's headlines covering the tragic event.

HORATIO SPAFFORD: *(HE enters from upstage right, reading the newspaper. HE spots the article and quickly reads.)*
"The Ocean Horror?" What in the world...?
(Reading.)
"Later details of the sinking of The Ville Du Havre. The vessel sunk on night of 23rd, over 200 souls drowned in mid-ocean... Names of the 87 saved..."
(HE looks on the next page and reads.)
Miss Mary Hunter... Rev. Nathanael Weiss... Mrs. H.G. Spafford..." Thank God. But where are my lambs? *(Frantically looking.)* No more? *(Beat.)* Oh, dear God.

MAIN NARRATOR: Seven days later, he received a telegram from Anna. It read:

[POWERPOINT of the telegram.]

HORATIO and ANNA: "Saved alone. What shall I do?"

HORATIO SPAFFORD: *(HE crosses to right of desk/ table, sets newspaper down on desk, removes hat, and sets it down.)*
I set off immediately to bring Anna home, and when my ship was crossing over the very place in the ocean...
(HORATIO crosses a bit downstage. MAIN NARRATOR as CAPTAIN starts his cross to him.)
...where our four daughters had perished, the captain notified me of our location.

[POWERPOINT goes to black.]

(MAIN NARRATOR as CAPTAIN points to location out front.)

HORATIO SPAFFORD: *(Looking out, then turns to MAIN NARRATOR as CAPTAIN.)*
Thank you.
(HORATIO steps downstage left a bit and looks out at the sea, over audience.)
But our dear ones are not here. They are safe, folded, with Jesus. *(Beat.)* I have never felt more like trusting God than I do now.
(GUITARIST/SINGER plays instrumental of "It Is Well With My Soul." HORATIO speaks the following lines in time with the guitar.)
"When peace like a river, attendeth my way, when sorrows like sea billows roll. Whatever my lot, thou hast taught me to say, 'It is well, it is well, with my soul.'"
(GUITARIST/SINGER fades out. HORATIO continues to address the audience.)
I returned to my cabin and wrote a hymn.
(HORATIO quickly crosses to the right of the desk/table, and sits.)
No doubt, I was inspired by those hymn writers who came before me—Luther, Newton, and countless others, but I also had scripture.
(HE picks up the Bible.)
The Apostle Paul suffered, too, and wrote these words to help guide us through *our* suffering.

MAIN NARRATOR: *(HE crosses downstage right.)*
> The Spaffords shared their testimony and the
> Good News message of the gospel to Chicago.

HORATIO SPAFFORD: *(HORATIO rises, with Bible in
> hand, as ANNA crosses into him, stopping
> downstage of the left of desk/table. HORATIO
> preaches to the audience as if they are the
> "Chicago audiences.")*
> "I have learned in whatever situation I am to be
> content. I know how to be brought low, and I
> know how to abound. In any and every
> circumstance, I have learned the secret of facing
> plenty and hunger, abundance and need. I can do
> all things through Him who strengthens me."
> *(HORATIO hands ANNA the Bible, and THEY
> share a look.)*

ANNA SPAFFORD: *(SHE, too, preaches to "Chicago
> audiences.")*
> I can do *all* things, not some things—*all* things
> through Christ who strengthens me. How do un-
> believers, people who do not have a personal
> relationship with Jesus Christ, how do they
> recognize authentic Christians?

HORATIO SPAFFORD: It isn't because we don't suffer,
> because God knows we do.

ANNA SPAFFORD: And it isn't because we behave
> perfectly in all situations...

HORATIO SPAFFORD: ...because I know, first-hand, I
> do not.

ANNA SPAFFORD: The Bible says, "You will know them
> by their fruits."

(ANNA sets Bible on table, and HORATIO and ANNA meet in front of the desk/table and take each other's hands.)

MAIN NARRATOR: The Spaffords founded the American Colony in Jerusalem...

[POWERPOINT of the Spaffords at the American Colony in Jerusalem.]

MAIN NARRATOR: *(Continuing.)* ...which ministered to the poor for many years. And by God's grace, Anna gave birth to three more children.

MAIN NARRATOR: *(The COUPLE separates. HORATIO sits in chair stage right of desk and quietly writes. ANNA crosses stage right, and MAIN NARRATOR crosses in.)*
But let's return to that cold day in November, on the deck of the Ville Du Havre, amidst those agonizing shrieks of people drowning, great disorder, panic, and terror... What did Anna do?

[POWERPOINT goes to black.]

(ANNA SPAFFORD gathers her four children, crosses downstage right, and kneels.)

MAIN NARRATOR: She led her four daughters to the main deck of that sinking ship, and together, they got down on their knees and prayed.
(GUITARIST/SINGER plays the introduction to "It is Well With My Soul." MAIN NARRATOR takes one more step downstage.)

When your world falls apart, where do you place your trust?

ANNA SPAFFORD: *(On her knees, praying.)*
God, if it could be your will, spare us. Or, if not, help us to endure what awaits us. We are completely in your hands.
(SHE buries her head in her hands.)

MAIN NARRATOR: When tragedy strikes, we go to Jesus because He will sustain us regardless of what comes our way. In spite of the great disorder, panic, and terror, Anna and her children got down on their knees, humbled themselves, and prayed with their hearts transfixed on Him. *(HE sits.)*

SONG: IT IS WELL

GUITARIST/SINGER & HORATIO: *(GUITARIST/SINGER rises and sings the song while Horatio, now turned in chair facing the audience with writing material in his lap, writes quickly as the song comes to him. HORATIO sings/speaks the lyrics while GUITARIST/SINGER sings the song traditionally.)*
MY SIN, OH, THE BLISS OF THIS GLORIOUS THOUGHT! MY SIN, NOT IN PART BUT THE WHOLE IS NAILED TO THE CROSS, AND I BEAR IT NO MORE. PRAISE THE LORD, PRAISE THE LORD, O MY SOUL!

GUITARIST/SINGER: IT IS WELL.

HORATIO: IT IS WELL.

GUITARIST/SINGER: WITH MY SOUL.

HORATIO: WITH MY SOUL.

BOTH: IT IS WELL, IT IS WELL WITH MY SOUL.

GUITARIST/SINGER: *(Sings verse 2, while HORATIO rises, puts on top hat, and picks up his luggage upstage of desk/table, with his left hand. ANNA rises and prepares to meet her husband at the "dock." SHE crosses further stage left.)*
AND LORD, HASTE THE DAY WHEN THE FAITH SHALL BE SIGHT.
(HORATIO prepares his overcoat.)
THE CLOUDS BE ROLLED BACK AS A SCROLL.
(HORATIO crosses downstage center, onto thrust, and passionately searches for ANNA, looking out over the audience on the "dock.")
THE TRUMP SHALL RESOUND, AND THE LORD SHALL DESCEND.
(HORATIO spots ANNA first.)
EVEN SO...

HORATIO: *(Calling out.)* Anna!
(HE crosses USL to her, with his suitcase still in his left hand, then sets the suitcase down, upstage of them.)

GUITARIST/SINGER: IT IS WELL WITH MY SOUL.
(HORATIO and ANNA embrace.)
IT IS WELL.

ANNA & HORATIO: *(Coming out of embrace, THEY hold each other's hands, facing each other.)*
IT IS WELL.

GUITARIST/SINGER: WITH MY SOUL.

ANNA & HORATIO: WITH MY SOUL.

GUITARIST/SINGER, HORATIO, AND ANNA:

> *(HORATIO and ANNA cross downstage center,*
> *holding hands.)*
>
> IT IS WELL; IT IS WELL WITH MY SOUL.
>
> *(MAIN NARRATOR rises.)*

GUITARIST/SINGER: IT IS WELL.

HORATIO, ANNA, AND MAIN NARRATOR:

> *(HORATIO and ANNA let go of each other's*
> *hands, and the three invite the audience to sing*
> *along.)*
>
> IT IS WELL.

GUITARIST/SINGER: WITH MY SOUL.

HORATIO, ANNA, AND MAIN NARRATOR:

> *(The three invite the audience to sing along.)*
>
> WITH MY SOUL.

EVERYONE: IT IS WELL, IT IS WELL WITH MY SOUL.

> IT IS WELL...
>
> *(HORATIO and ANNA take hands once more,*
> *sharing a fond exchange.)*
>
> IT IS WELL WITH MY SOUL.
>
> *(LIGHTS OUT. MAIN NARRATOR, HORATIO,*
> *and ANNA exit upstage right. In the dark,*
> *LONGFELLOW NARRATOR enters and removes*
> *luggage from upstage left and exits upstage left.)*

End of Scene

ACT TWO

Scene 2
"'Tis So Sweet to Trust in Jesus"
- 1882 -

(LOUISA M. R. STEAD enters in the dark, places basket downstage right, and lays a blanket over the back of the stage right desk/table chair. SHE picks up newer Bible from desk/table, and stands right of desk/table. LIGHTS UP on LOUISA reading from Bible with an English accent.)

LOUISA M. R. STEAD: "Behold, God is my salvation; I will trust, and will not be afraid; for the Lord God is my strength and my song, and he has become my salvation."
(SHE takes the Bible's ribbon and marks her place, retrieves the blanket, then crosses downstage right.)
It was a beautiful, sunny day on Long Island Sound. My husband and I decided to go for a picnic on the beach with our daughter, Lily.
(SHE opens up the blanket, flips it out, and watches it fall onto the stage. SHE looks out over the water/audience and takes a deep breath.)
It was lovely.
(SHE sets basket onto blanket and sits.)

I had arranged the perfect lunch, and we were enjoying it together when suddenly we heard screaming...
(SHE comes up onto her knees.)
...a young boy screaming out amongst the waves. My husband, kind, compassionate, without a thought of himself, raced into the surf to save him. But, as often happens in these situations, the struggling boy, with flailing arms, pulled his rescuer down. *(Beat.)* And there we sat, me and our four-year-old daughter, watching helplessly as they both drowned.
(SHE rises.)
I have decided that good things happen slow...
(SHE places basket on large trunk.)
...but bad things?
(SHE picks up blanket in one movement and holds it to her.)
Well...bad things happen fast, don't they? And sometimes when bad things start happening, they don't stop. Without my husband, we became extremely poor extremely fast. And yet, looking back, God provided for us, and we somehow made it through.
(SHE folds the blanket as GUITARIST/SINGER plays the music to the words: "'Tis so Sweet to Trust in Jesus...")
"Behold, God is my salvation..."
(GUITARIST/SINGER plays music to the words "...just to take him at his word.")
"I will trust and will not be afraid..."

(GUITARIST/SINGER plays "Just to rest upon his promise.")

"...for the Lord God is my strength and *my song*..."

(GUITARIST/SINGER plays "Just to know, 'Thus sayeth the Lord.'")

My song.

(SHE points upward.)

He is my song.

(SHE places blanket on the large trunk and crosses to right of desk/table. GUITARIST/ SINGER plays instrumental guitar softly and slowly as LOUISA sits at the writing table and writes her song. SHE speaks the words as SHE writes.)

"'Tis so sweet to trust in Jesus, and to take him at his word. Just to rest upon his promise. Just to know, 'Thus sayeth the Lord.'"

(GUITARIST/SINGER fades out. LOUISA rises and steps downstage of desk/table.)

[POWERPOINT of the White Cliffs of Dover.]

LOUISA M. R. STEAD: *(Continuing.)*

Has anyone ever been to the White Cliffs of Dover, England? They're beautiful, aren't they? I was born there, in Dover, in 1850. At age 9, I accepted Christ, and at age 21, I immigrated to the United States. In 1875, I married. I've always had frail health, but for as long as I can remember I wanted to be a missionary. So, after I

lost my husband, my trust in Jesus became
stronger than my ill health. My daughter and I
sold everything we owned, which wasn't much,
packed our bags, and moved to South Africa
where we...*became missionaries*! *(Beat.)*
God may allow challenges in our lives, but He is
the great comforter, and in time, the ones who
suffer, having been comforted by God himself,
can then comfort others with that same comfort.
*(SHE crosses upstage to the right of the desk/
table and lifts up her book.)*
My little hymn was published in 1882 by the
National Publishing Association in the
hymnal *Songs of Triumph.*
(Opens book and reads.)
"Louisa M. R. Stead." It is my hope that the
writing of these words helps others deal with
tragedy like mine. My theme? *(Beat.)* Simple.
Trust in Jesus.
*(GUITARIST/SINGER plays the introduction to
song, "'Tis So Sweet to Trust in Jesus" – Key of
F.)*

SONG: 'TIS SO SWEET TO TRUST IN JESUS

LOUISA M. R. STEAD: *(SHE crosses downstage onto
the thrust, stage right of thrust, singing.)*
TIS SO SWEET TO TRUST IN JESUS
AND TO TAKE HIM AT HIS WORD
JUST TO REST UPON HIS PROMISE
AND TO KNOW, "THUS SAITH THE LORD."

JESUS, JESUS, HOW I TRUST HIM!
HOW I'VE PROVED HIM O'ER AND O'ER!
JESUS, JESUS, PRECIOUS JESUS!
O FOR GRACE TO TRUST HIM MORE!
(SHE crosses stage left on thrust, singing.)
O HOW SWEET TO TRUST IN JESUS,
JUST TO TRUST HIS CLEANSING BLOOD
AND IN SIMPLE FAITH TO PLUNGE ME
'NEATH THE HEALING, CLEANSING FLOOD!

LOUISA M. R. STEAD and GUITARIST/SINGER:
(Singing.)
JESUS, JESUS, HOW I TRUST HIM!
HOW I'VE PROVED HIM O'ER AND O'ER!
JESUS, JESUS, PRECIOUS JESUS!
O FOR GRACE TO TRUST HIM MORE!
(SHE crosses upstage, retrieves the OLD Bible from the desk/table, and holds it to her chest.)

GUITARIST/SINGER: I'M SO GLAD I LEARNED TO TRUST THEE.

LOUISA M. R. STEAD: PRECIOUS JESUS, SAVIOR, FRIEND.
(SHE crosses stage right.)

GUITARIST/SINGER: AND I KNOW THAT THOU ART WITH ME.

LOUISA M. R. STEAD: WILT BE WITH ME TO THE END.

LOUISA and ANNA: *(ANNA enters singing, crosses to stand to the left of Louisa.)* JESUS, JESUS...

LOUISA, ANNA, and LONGFELLOW NARRATOR: *(LN enters singing, crosses to stand downstage left.)* ...HOW I TRUST HIM!

LOUISA, ANNA, LONGFELLOW NARRATOR, and
HORATIO: *(HORATIO enters singing, crosses to stand left of Anna.)*
> HOW I'VE PROVED...

LOUISA, ANNA, LONGFELLOW NARRATOR,
HORATIO, and JOHN NEWTON: *(JOHN NEWTON enters singing, crosses to stand far stage left, nearest to Guitarist/Singer.)*
> ...HIM O'ER AND O'ER!

LOUISA, ANNA, LONGFELLOW NARRATOR,
HORATIO, JOHN NEWTON, and MAIN NARRATOR:
> *(MAIN NARRATOR enters singing, crosses to stand downstage center.)*
> JESUS, JESUS, PRECIOUS JESUS!
> *(THEY are all standing across the stage in a line.)*

EVERYONE: *(LOUISA hands Bible to ANNA.)*
> OH FOR GRACE...

EVERYONE: *(ANNA hands Bible to HORATIO.)*
> OH FOR GRACE...

EVERYONE: *(HORATIO hands Bible to MAIN NARRATOR.)*
> OH FOR GRACE...

EVERYONE: *(MAIN NARRATOR hands Bible to LONGFELLOW NARRATOR.)*
> TO TRUST...

EVERYONE: *(LONGFELLOW NARRATOR hands Bible to JOHN NEWTON.)*
> ...HIM MORE.

JOHN NEWTON: *(The song ends, applause, then JOHN NEWTON hands the Old Bible to the GUITARIST/SINGER.)*

Your turn.

(EVERYONE encourages him, and the GUITARIST/SINGER accepts the challenge. HE takes the Bible and rises, with the guitar still around his neck.)

GUITARIST/SINGER: I was born in 2003.

(Beat.)

Guess I don't fit in with the others in that regard. I grew up listening to, playing, and singing their songs. And now...*I, too, write* Christian worship songs. I enjoy worshiping God through my music. My name is Max Horsewood, and I am a Christian songwriter and guitarist.

(HE hands the Bible back to JOHN NEWTON, who places it on the desk/table, then GUITARIST/SINGER crosses stage right a bit.)

Over a year ago, the high schoolers of my home church went on a mission trip to a kid's summer camp...without me. But when they got back, they told me that a group of them had gotten together and put Psalm 17 to music, word for word. That greatly interested me—taking words right out of the Bible and putting them to music, so I thought maybe I would try it. I started pairing scripture with melody to see if something "resembling a song" could result, and I found that it worked for *more* than just Psalm 17. And the songs started to pour out of me.

(JOHN NEWTON gently pushes GUITARIST/ SINGER from behind to take the stage and share his own music. EVERYONE encourages him. So, GUITARIST/SINGER crosses DSC onto thrust.)

This one was *inspired* by Hebrews 10 through 12, where God himself speaks to his people, exhorting them to continue in the faith with strong assurance, a healthy fear of Him, and hope for a great reward, and...*it was written by me.*

SONG: UNTIL WE BEHOLD HIS FACE

GUITARIST/SINGER: *(HE sings and plays his new, original song in the key of G.)*
   IN A LITTLE WHILE
   HE WHO COMES WILL COME.
   HE WILL NOT WAIT.
   AND THE RIGHTEOUS WILL LIVE BY FAITH
   IF HE SHRINKS BACK.
   MY SOUL...
EVERYONE: *(Echoing.)* MY SOUL.
GUITARIST/SINGER: HAS NO PLEASURE IN HIM.
   MY SOUL...
EVERYONE: *(Echoing.)* MY SOUL.
GUITARIST/SINGER: HAS NO PLEASURE IN HIM.
   (GUITARIST/SINGER repeats all the above in the higher octave while EVERYONE claps in time with him. HE crosses downstage right on thrust; EVERYONE stops clapping.)

BUT WE ARE NOT OF THOSE WHO SHRINK
BACK TO BE DESTROYED. OH NO, NO.
WE ARE THE FAITHFUL ONES WHO
PRESERVE THEIR SOULS *(Crosses to center.)*
LOOKING TO JESUS...

EVERYONE: LOOKING TO JESUS.

GUITARIST/SINGER: BEGINNING AND END OF OUR
FAITH. LET'S RUN WITH ENDURANCE...

EVERYONE: RUN WITH ENDURANCE.

GUITARIST/SINGER: UNTIL WE BEHOLD HIS FACE.
LOOKING TO JESUS...

EVERYONE: LOOKING TO JESUS.

GUITARIST/SINGER: BEGINNING AND END OF OUR
FAITH. LET'S RUN WITH ENDURANCE...

EVERYONE: RUN WITH ENDURANCE.

GUITARIST/SINGER: UNTIL WE BEHOLD HIS FACE.
(EVERYONE claps.)
THROWING OFF EVERY WEIGHT
SURROUNDED BY ALL GOD'S SAINTS
WE SHALL RUN AND NOT GROW FAINT
LET'S RUN WITH ENDURANCE.

EVERYONE: *(Echoing.)*
RUN WITH ENDURANCE.

GUITARIST/SINGER: THROWING OFF EVERY
WEIGHT. SURROUNDED BY ALL GOD'S
SAINTS. WE SHALL RUN AND NOT GROW
FAINT. LET'S RUN WITH ENDURANCE.

EVERYONE: *(Echoing.)* RUN WITH ENDURANCE.

GUITARIST/SINGER: LET'S RUN WITH ENDURANCE

EVERYONE: *(Echoing.)* RUN WITH ENDURANCE.

GUITARIST/SINGER: LET'S RUN WITH ENDURANCE

EVERYONE: *(Echoing.)* RUN WITH ENDURANCE.

GUITARIST/SINGER: LET'S RUN WITH
ENDURANCE.

(EVERYONE stops clapping.)

GUITARIST/SINGER: LOOKING TO JESUS...

EVERYONE: *(Echoing.)* LOOKING TO JESUS.

GUITARIST/SINGER: THE BEGINNING AND END OF
OUR FAITH. LET'S RUN WITH ENDURANCE...

EVERYONE: RUN WITH ENDURANCE.

GUITARIST/SINGER: UNTIL WE BEHOLD HIS FACE.

(Song ends.)

Thank you.

JOHN NEWTON: And the stories of faith continue as
we "run with endurance the race that is set before
us." *(Beat.)* Thank you, young man. That was...
inspired! (Beat.) And, for the record, I have ties
older than you.

*(LONGFELLOW NARRATOR and HORATIO
SPAFFORD put on their guitars.)*

JOHN NEWTON: This evening, you've heard stories of
how God worked through these individuals, these
imperfect people. But when *you* walk in Christ,
He leads you to and through what you've been
called to do.

(The following lines flow without hesitation.)

GUITARIST/SINGER: So, "Trust in the Lord with all
your heart, and do not lean on your own
understanding." *[Proverbs 3:5]*

LOUISA M. R. STEAD: "In all your ways acknowledge
Him, and He will direct your paths." *[Proverbs
3:6]*

HORATIO: "Do not be wise in your *own* eyes." *[Proverbs 3:7]*

ANNA: "For His thoughts are not your thoughts, neither are *your* ways *His* ways." *[Isaiah 55:8]*

LONGFELLOW NARRATOR: "When I am afraid, I put my trust in Him." *[Psalm 56:3]*

JOHN NEWTON: Because "I can do all things through Christ who strengthens me." *[Phil. 4:13]*

MAIN NARRATOR: "For His power is made perfect in my weakness." *[2 Corinthians 12:9]*

HORATIO: "You are from God and have overcome the world, for He who is in you is greater than he who is in the world." *[1 John 4:4]*

LONGFELLOW NARRATOR: So we ask you, when you walk out of this theatre tonight *[this afternoon]*, do not take the old doubting self with you. After all, it's not YOU you have to trust. It's Jesus.

SONG: THE BLESSING

LONGFELLOW NARRATOR: *(HORATIO, GUITARIST/ SINGER, and LN all play the song on their guitars, but LN sings the first verse by herself. Capo is on the first fret.)*
THE LORD BLESS YOU AND KEEP YOU.
MAKE HIS FACE SHINE UPON YOU, AND BE GRACIOUS TO YOU.
THE LORD TURN HIS FACE TOWARD YOU AND GIVE YOU PEACE.

LN AND GUITARIST/SINGER: *(GS sings melody, and LM sings harmony.)*

THE LORD BLESS YOU AND KEEP YOU.
MAKE HIS FACE SHINE UPON YOU, AND BE
GRACIOUS TO YOU.
THE LORD TURN HIS FACE TOWARD YOU
AND GIVE YOU PEACE.

EVERYONE: *(EVERYONE on melody.)*
A-MEN. A-MEN, A-MEN.
(LN sings harmony. EVERYONE else stays on melody.)
A-MEN. A-MEN, A-MEN.

LONGFELLOW NARRATOR and LOUISA STEAD:
MAY HIS FAVOR BE UPON YOU, AND A
THOUSAND GENERATIONS
AND YOUR FAMILY AND YOUR CHILDREN,
AND THEIR CHILDREN, AND THEIR
CHILDREN.

LM, LOUISA, and GUITARIST/SINGER:
(GS comes in on melody, and LN/LOUISA sing harmony.)
MAY HIS PRESENCE GO BEFORE YOU, AND
BEHIND YOU, AND BESIDE YOU
ALL AROUND YOU, AND WITHIN YOU, HE IS
WITH YOU, HE IS WITH YOU
(GS, LM, and LOUISA go up a step.)
IN THE MORNING, IN THE EVENING, IN
YOUR COMING, AND YOUR GOING
IN YOUR WEEPING, AND REJOICING, HE IS
FOR YOU, HE IS FOR YOU
(GUITARIST/SINGER extends note while LN continues.)
HE IS FOR YOU; HE IS FOR YOU.

HE IS FOR YOU; HE IS FOR YOU.
HE IS FOR YOU; HE IS FOR YOU.
HE IS FOR YOU; HE IS FOR YOU.
EVERYONE: *(Together.)*
A-MEN. A-MEN, A-MEN
LONGFELLOW NARRATOR & EVERYONE: *(LN goes up. EVERYONE else stays the same.)*
A-MEN. A-MEN, A-MEN
LONGFELLOW NARRATOR: *(All three guitars continue to play, but only LN sings.)*
THE LORD BLESS YOU, AND KEEP YOU
MAKE HIS FACE SHINE UPON YOU, AND BE
GRACIOUS TO YOU.
LONGFELLOW NARRATOR and GUITARIST/SINGER: *(LN continues to sing melody; GS sings melody.)*
THE LORD TURN HIS, FACE TOWARD YOU
AND GIVE YOU PEACE.

(Curtain call, then LIGHTS FADE out.)

End of Play

PROPERTIES

FURNITURE PRESET ONSTAGE

- Middle-sized antique-looking table downstage center, with room to walk downstage of it.
- Two chairs on either side of the table.
- Large trunk, stage right.
- Podium downstage right w/bullhorn masked beneath it.
- Two guitar stands/2 guitars/chair/small trunk, stage left.
- Framed painting of a boat in trouble, 2' x 3', hanging upstage center, far above the table. The original production used "Christ in the Storm on the Sea of Galilee" by Rembrandt.
- There are two wings, 7.5' x 8.6', with gold curtains, one on either side of the stage for actors to be masked when not on stage.

PROPS ON TABLE DOWNSTAGE CENTER

- Tablecloth, lantern, pewter mug, sheet music, two inkwells (one throwable), two feather pens, Victorian fan for Longfellow piece, and two Victorian pens.
- Books: Warner Sister's *Say and Seal*, *Longfellow*, New Bible, Old Bible, Louisa's Hymnbook, Newton's slavery book.

PROPS OFFSTAGE RIGHT

- Newspaper & guitar on stand for Horatio Spafford.
- Blanket & Basket for Louisa Stead.
- Longfellow book for Longfellow Narrator.

PERSONAL PROPS

- Knife in the pocket for John Newton.
- Two pitch pipes for the two Monks.

BETWEEN ACTS

- Remove the podium and bullhorn.
- Place suitcase upstage of desk/table.

(Cast of the original production in rehearsal: Max Horsewood, Greg Helton, Lisa Soland, Kris Phillips, Joe Casterline, Jeannine Brown, and Christiane Frith. Photo by Stefan Holt.)

(Christiane Frith played the *Warner Sisters Narrator,* and Joe Casterline was the *Schoolteacher*. Photo by Steven Wilson.)

(Lisa Soland plays the guitar as *Longfellow Narrator*, and Max Horsewood as *Guitarist/Singer/Songwriter*.
Photo by Steven Wilson.)

(Original cast in costume: Kris Phillips, Lisa Soland, Greg Helton, Joe Casterline, Christiane Frith, Jeannine Brown, and Max Horsewood. Photo by Steven Wilson.)

Notes from the Playwright/Director

In the original production of *Inspired!*, we discovered that the PowerPoint images increased the sense of realism in the stories, which had a more significant impact on the audience. We had access to two permanent screens above the stage, right and left. If you are using a space that does not already have PowerPoint screens, you can purchase a freestanding screen and place it on the stage. But you have my blessing if making that happen for your show is financially challenging.

We built two freestanding vintage-like curtains supported by PVC pipe and placed them upstage right and left. However, when we traveled off-site with the show, we found that most facilities did not have a built-in screen. So, we used only one of our two curtains for those shows and placed that upstage right. We then purchased a PowerPoint screen and projector, and placed those upstage left. We hung the ship painting center on the upstage right curtain. If this is your plan, I recommend making a curtain for the lower portion of your PowerPoint screen using the same material used to build your upstage right curtain. Our material was a thick, rich yellow color. Using matching curtain material for your PVC curtain upstage right and for the lower portion of your PowerPoint screen stage left will help maintain the illusion that we are in the 1500s to the 1800s.

For the original production, the GUITARIST/SINGER was also a Christian songwriter. The concept for the premiere of *Inspired!* was to use an actual musician/singer/songwriter and tell their actual, true story. It would be ideal to use such a person if they exist in your community. The MUSICIAN/SINGER acts as the "pit band" and occupies the space far stage left. Make sure that their "introduction-to-the-song" monologue is brief and scripted. Please do not allow them to improvise.

Though certainly to the audience, it should appear as if they are improvising. If your musician/singer is not also a Christian songwriter, use the monologue and song we have provided in this script (originally written and performed by Max Horsewood).

As you know, all of this material for *Inspired!* is copyrighted and must be performed precisely as written. You must obtain a licensing agreement to use any of it. We want to thank Max Horsewood for his fine job arranging the music. We have included his work in this script for your convenience, but again, this is all copyrighted material. To obtain "Rights and Permissions," the author or their representative may be contacted at AllOriginalPlays@gmail.com. For more details, refer to the copyright page at the front of this publication.

A Mighty Fortress

Acoustic Guitar

Martin Luther

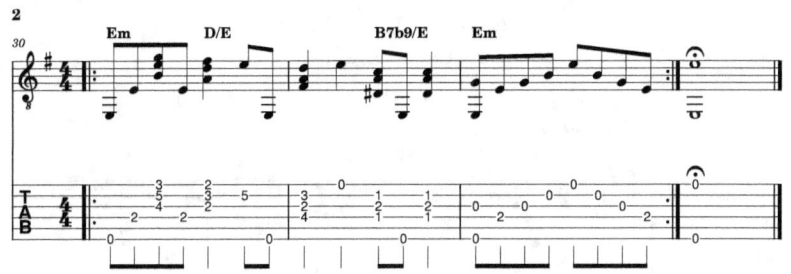

Amazing Grace

No Capo - Key of E

John Newton

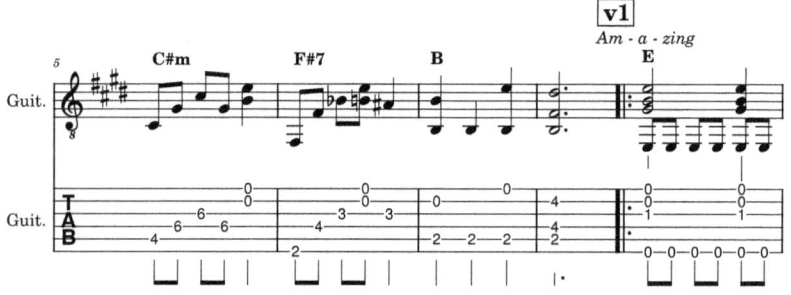

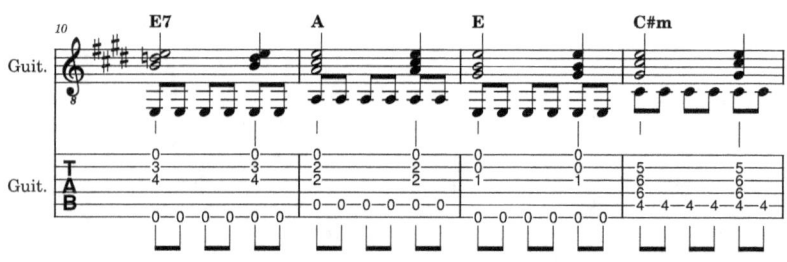

Interlude

My memory is nearly gone...

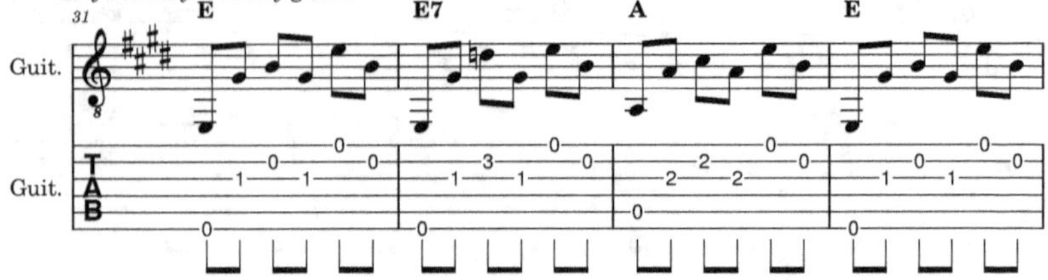

v3 *The Lord has promised good to me...*

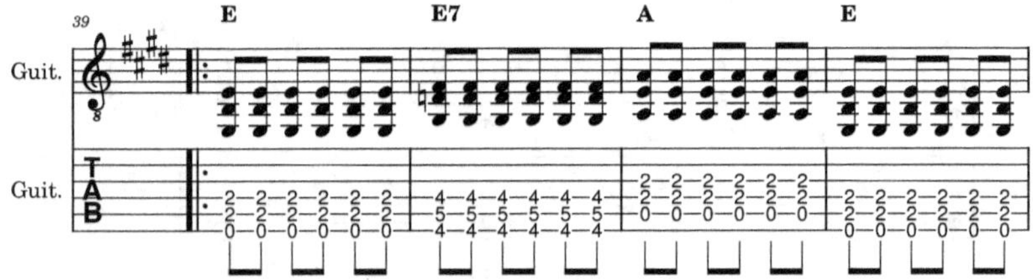

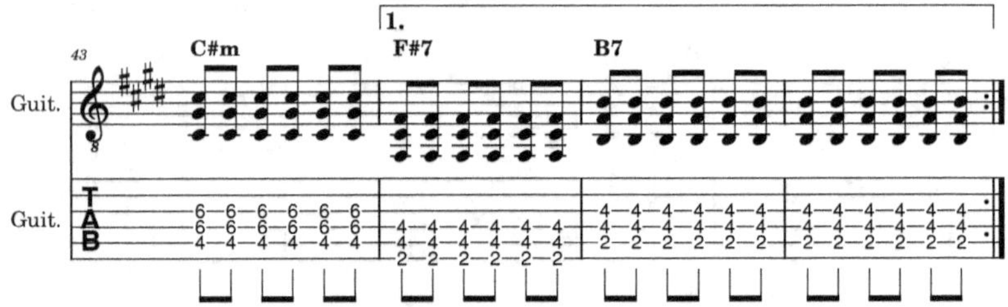

4

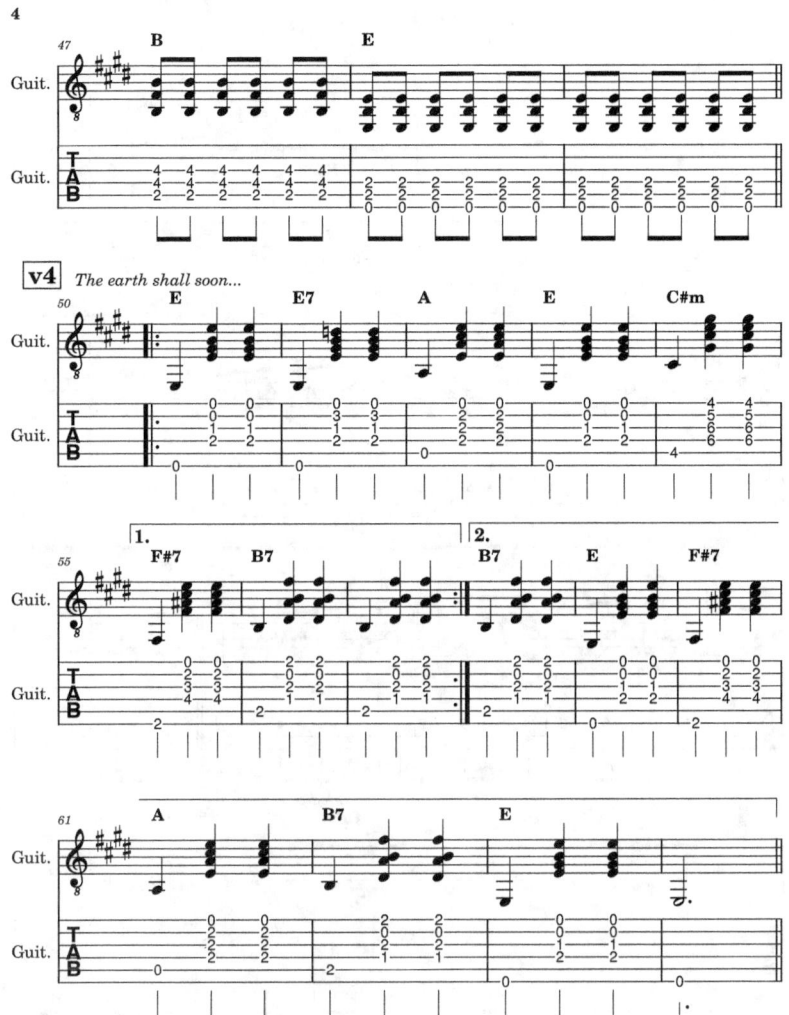

v4 *The earth shall soon...*

Jesus Loves Me

Capo 2 - Key of A

Susan Warner

2

Jesus loves me...

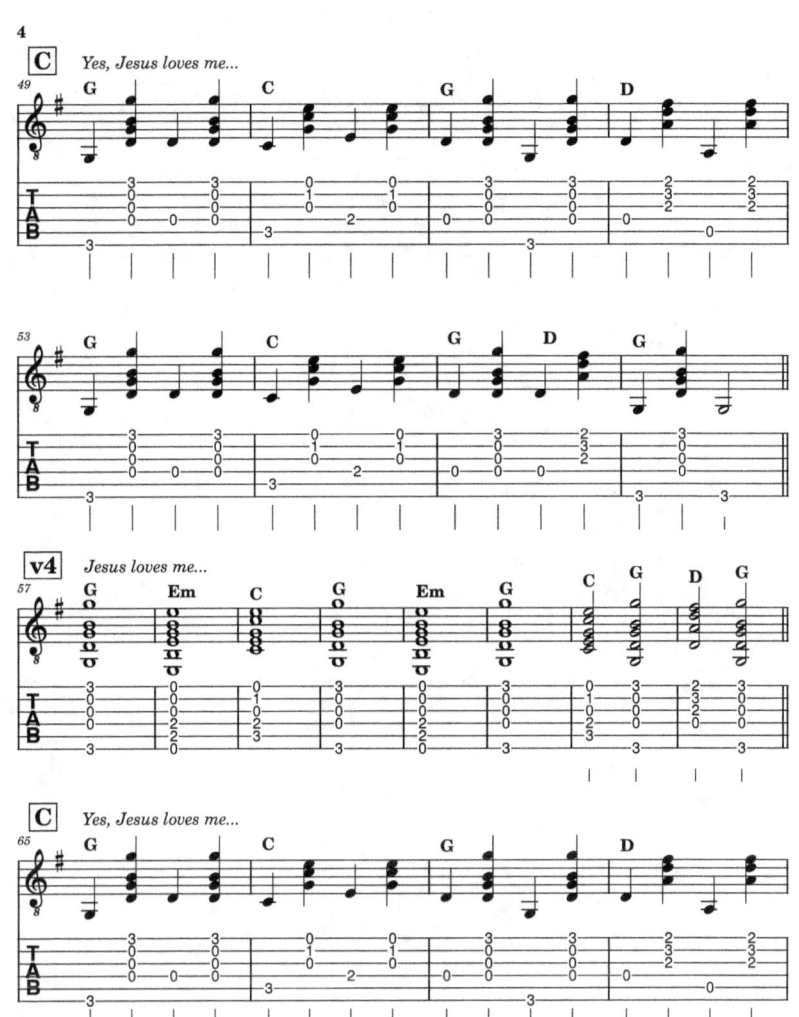

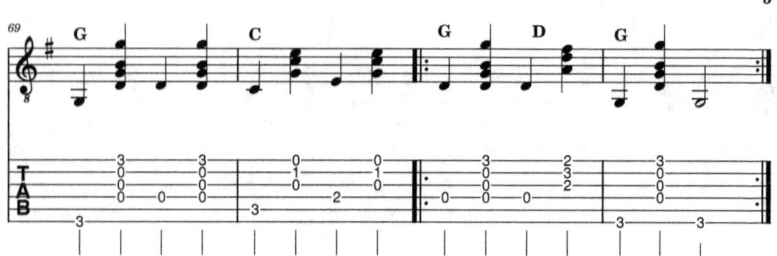

Battle Hymn / I Heard The Bells

Capo 4 (For both songs)

Henry Wadsworth Longfellow

Swing ♩ = 75

*Tragedy was not over
for this family...*

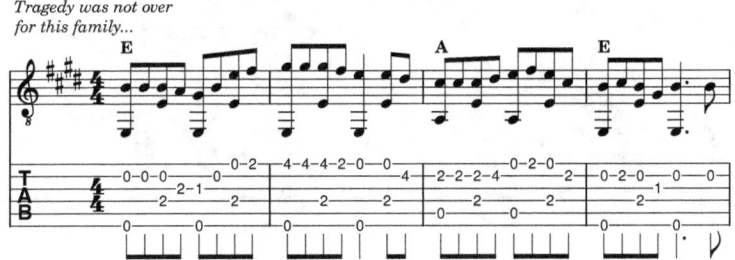

Paralyzed for life...

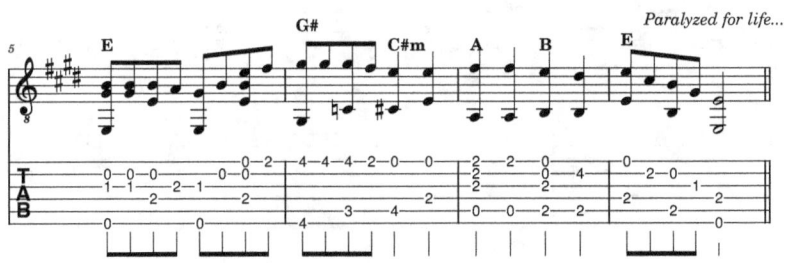

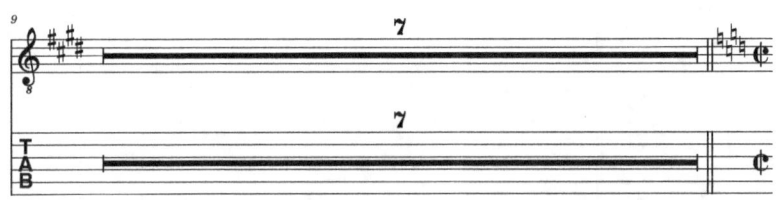

2

Straight ♩ = 45   *He heard the ringing of*
                   the town's Christmas bells...

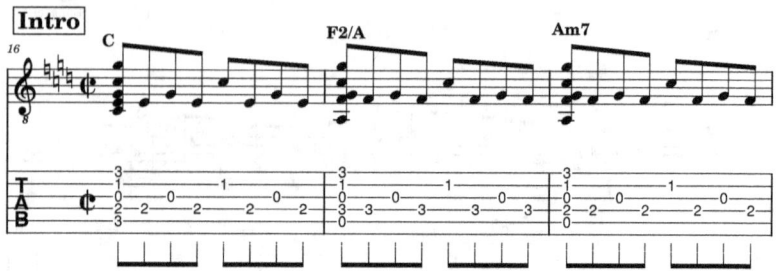

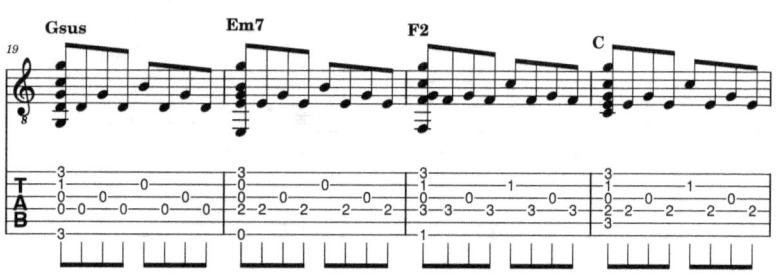

I heard the bells on Christmas day...

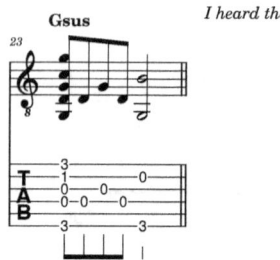

I Heard the Bells on Christmas Day

Capo 4

```
C                    Dm
I heard the bells on Christmas day
     C/E        F      Gsus
Their old familiar carols play,
        C              E7      Am
And wild and sweet the words repeat
    C                 G7    C
Of peace on earth, good will to men.
```

```
 C                    Dm
I thought how, as the day had come,
     C/E        F      Gsus
The belfries of all Christendom
        C              E7      Am
Had rolled along the unbroken song
    C                 G7    C
Of peace on earth, good will to men.
```

```
    Am          Dm
And in despair I bowed my head:
        C          F      Gsus   G
"There is no peace on earth," I said,
        C              E7      Am
"For hate is strong and mocks the song
    C                 G     C     Asus   A
Of peace on earth, good will to men."
```

```
     D                    Em
Then pealed the bells more loud and deep:
     D/F#         G      Asus    A
"God is not dead, nor doth he sleep;
        D               F#    Bm    Bm/G#
The wrong shall fail, the right prevail,
        D              E7
With peace on earth, with peace on earth
        D              A7     D
With peace on earth, good will to men."
```

It Is Well With My Soul

Capo 2 - Key of A

Use Fingerstyle pattern or strum light chords

Horatio Spafford

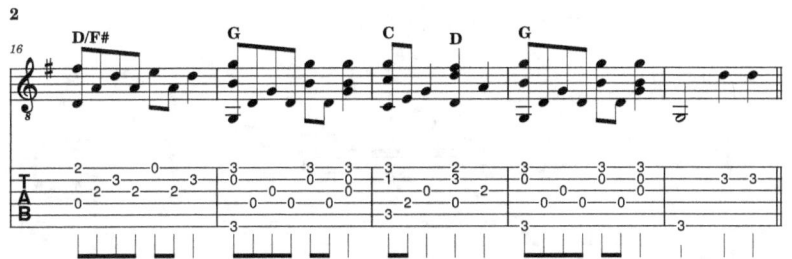

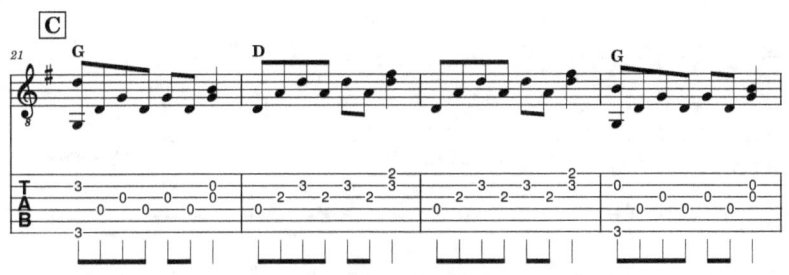

Tis So Sweet To Trust In Jesus

Capo 3 - Key of Eb

Louisa Stead

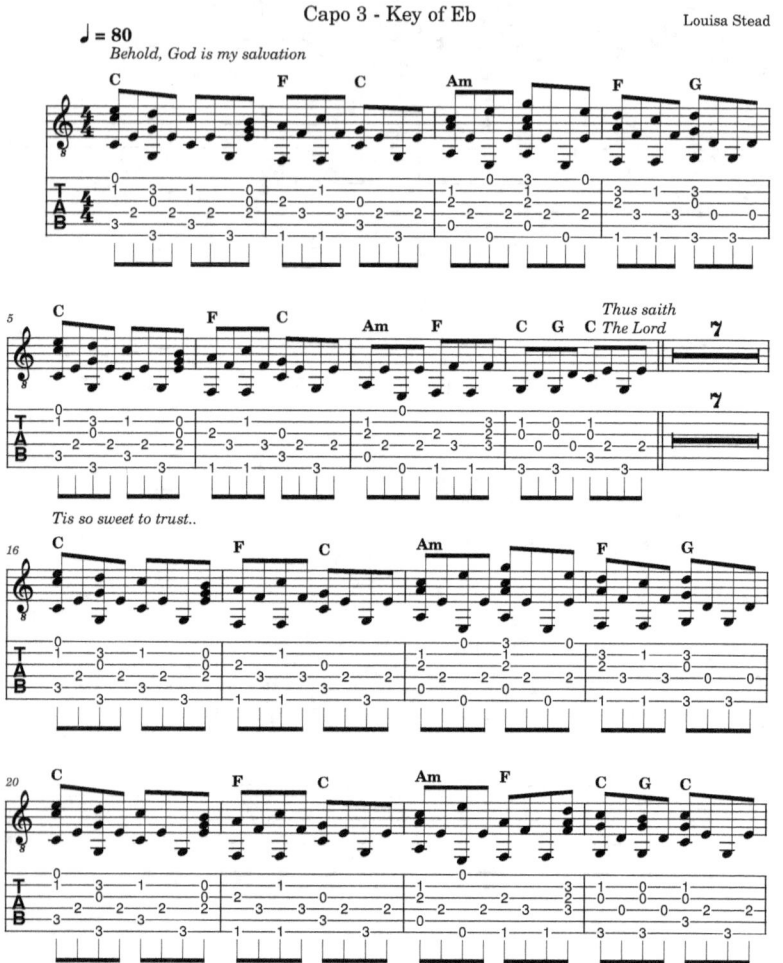

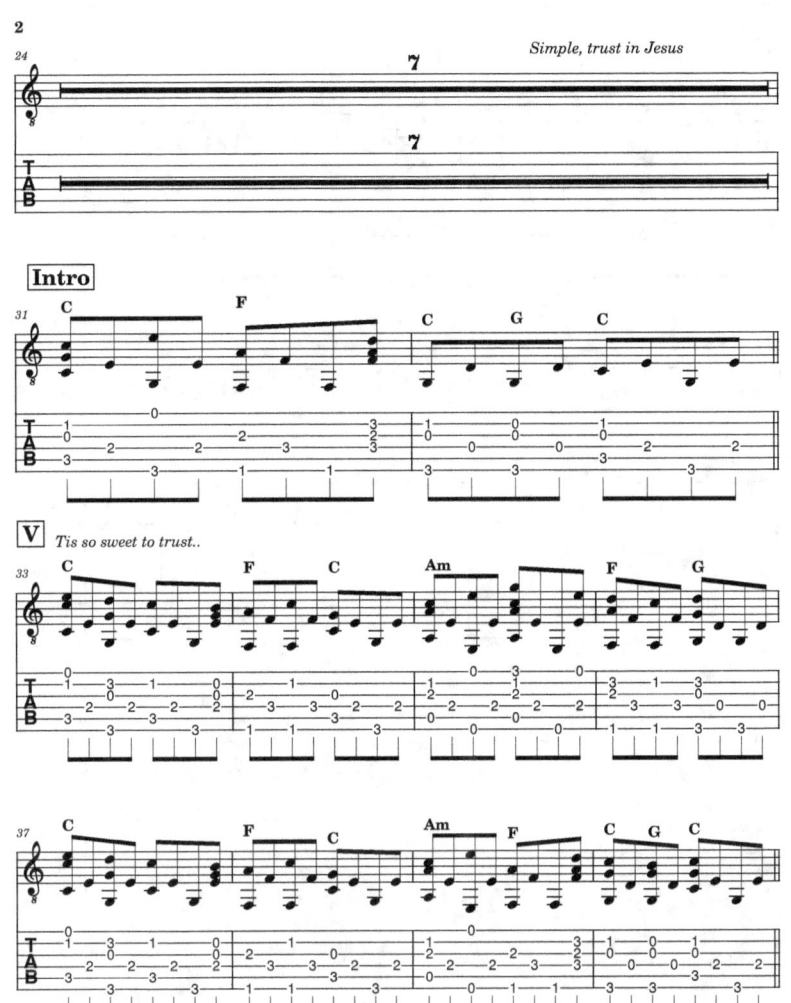

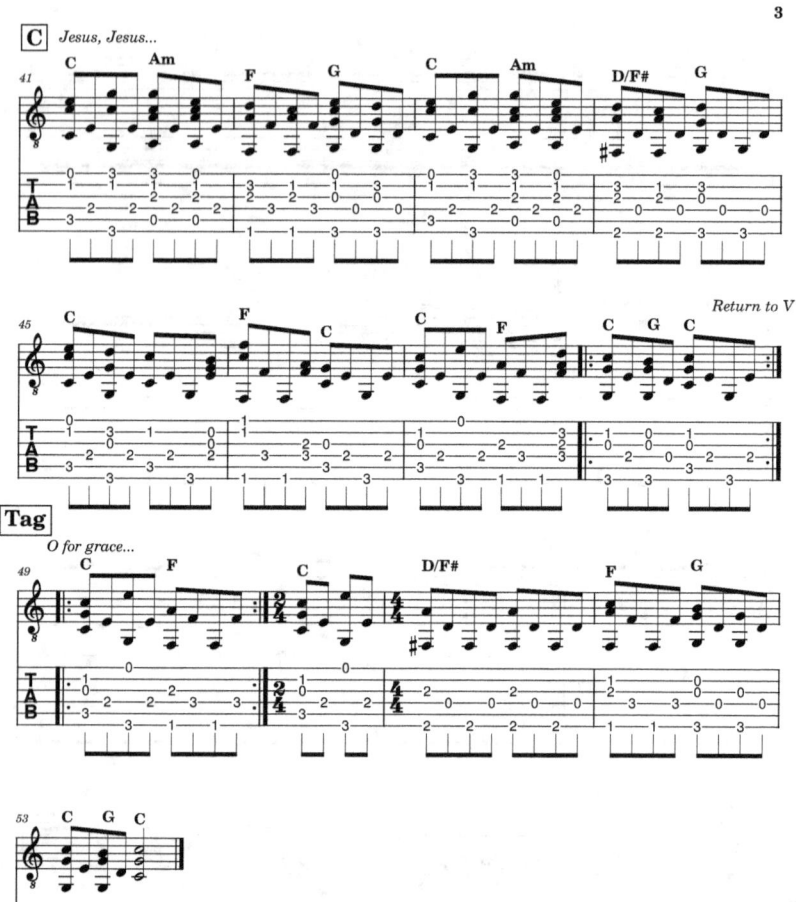

3

Looking To Jesus

Based on Hebrews

Max Horsewood

2

Bridge

throw-ing off__ ev__ ry__ weight surr-oun__ ded by__ all__ God's saints we

__ shall run__ and not__ grow faint let's run with en – dur__ ance

Tag 2

run with en – dur__ ance__ let's run with en – dur__ ance__

run with en – dur____ ance____

Chorus

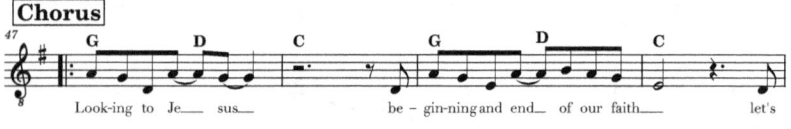

Look-ing to Je__ sus__ be – gin-ning and end__ of our faith__ let's

run with en – dur__ ance__ un – til we be – hold__ his__ face____

The Blessing

Acoustic Guitar Intro / Outro
Key of Ab / Capo 6

Cody Carnes / Chris Brown /
Steven Furtick / Kari Jobe Carnes

Until We Behold His Face [G]

[Default Arrangement]

Intro
G / / D / / | C / / / | G / / D / / | C / / /

Verse
G / D / C / / /   G /   D /   C / / /
In a little while, he who comes will come and will not wait
G /   D /   C / / /   G /   D /   C / / /
But the righteous will live by faith, and if he shrinks back
   Em / D / C / / /   Em /   D /   C / / /
My soul   has no pleasure in him
   Em / D / C / / /   Em /   D /   C / / /
My soul   has no pleasure in him

Prechorus
Bm /   C /   D /   Em /   C /   G / | D / / /
But we are not of those who shrink back to be destroyed
Bm /   C /   D /   Em /   C /   G / | D / / /
We are the faithful ones who preserve their souls

Chorus (x2)
G /   D /   C / / / G /   D /   C / / /
Looking to Jesus ,   beginning and end of our faith
     G /   D /   C / / / G /   D /   C / / /
Let's run with endurance   until we behold his face

Bridge
Em /   D / C / G /   Em /   D / C /   G /
Throwing off ev'ry weight, surrounded by all God's saints
Em /   D /   C /   G /
We shall run and not grow faint
    C /
Let's run with endurance

Bridge
Em /   D / C / G /   Em /   D / C /   G /
Throwing off ev'ry weight, surrounded by all God's saints
Em /   D /   C /   G /
We shall run and not grow faint
    Cmaj7 / / / | / / / /
Let's run with endurance
     A7/C# / / / | / / / /
Let's run with endurance
    Cmaj7 / / / | / / / /
Let's run with endurance
     A7/C# / / /   C/D / / /
Let's run with endurance

Chorus (x2)
G /   D /   C / / / G /   D /   C / / /
Looking to Jesus ,   beginning and end of our faith
     G /   D /   C / / / G /   D /   C / / /   (Song end on G)
Let's run with endurance   until we behold his face

1

Until We Behold His Face [E]

[Default Arrangement]

Intro
E / / B / / | A / / / | E / / B / / | A / / /

Verse
E /   B /   A / / /   E /   B /   A / / /
In a little while, he who comes will come and will not wait
E /   B /   A / / /   E /   B /   A / / /
But the righteous will live by faith, and if he shrinks back
   C#m /B / A / / /   C#m /   B /   A / / /
My soul   has no pleasure in him
   C#m /B / A / / /   C#m /   B /   A / / /
My soul   has no pleasure in him

Prechorus
G#m /   A /   B /   C#m /   A /   E / | B / / /
But we are not of those who shrink back to be destroyed
G#m /   A /   B /   C#m /   A / E / | B / / /
We are the faithful ones who preserve their souls

Chorus (x2)
E /   B /   A / / /   E /   B /   A / / /
Looking to Jesus ,   beginning and end of our faith
     E /   B /   A / / / E /   B /   A / / /
Let's run with endurance   until we behold his face

Bridge
C#m /   B / A /   E /   C#m /   B / A /   E /
Throwing off ev'ry weight, surrounded by all God's saints
C#m /   B /   A /   E /
We shall run and not grow faint
       A /
Let's run with endurance

Bridge
C#m /   B / A /   E /   C#m /   B / A /   E /
Throwing off ev'ry weight, surrounded by all God's saints
C#m /   B /   A /   E /
We shall run and not grow faint
     Amaj7 / / / | / / / /
Let's run with endurance
     F#7/A# / / / | / / / /
Let's run with endurance
     Amaj7 / / / | / / / /
Let's run with endurance
     F#7/A# / / /   A/B / / /
Let's run with endurance

Chorus (x2)
E /   B /   A / / /   E /   B /   A / / /
Looking to Jesus ,   beginning and end of our faith
     E /   B /   A / / / E /   B /   A / / /   (Song end on G)
Let's run with endurance   until we behold his face

1

"Until We Behold His Face" composed by Max Horsewood
© *Max Horsewood*

Until We Behold His Face [D]

[Default Arrangement]

Intro
D / / A / / | G / / / | D / / A / / | G / / /

Verse
D / A / G / / /   D /   A /   G / / /
In a little while, he who comes will come and will not wait
D /   A /   G / / /   D /   A /   G / / /
But the righteous will live by faith, and if he shrinks back
   Bm / A / G / / /   Bm /   A /   G / / /
My soul   has no pleasure in him
   Bm / A / G / / /   Bm /   A /   G / / /
My soul   has no pleasure in him

Prechorus
F#m /   G /   A /   Bm /   G /   D / | A / / /
But we are not of those who shrink back to be destroyed
F#m /   G /   A /   Bm /   G /   D / | A / / /
We are the faithful ones who preserve their souls

Chorus (x2)
D /   A /   G / / / D /   A /   G / / /
Looking to Jesus ,   beginning and end of our faith
    D /   A /   G / / / D /   A /   G / / /
Let's run with endurance   until we behold his face

Bridge
Bm /   A / G / D /   Bm /   A / G /   D /
Throwing off ev'ry weight, surrounded by all God's saints
Bm /   A /   G /   D /
We shall run and not grow faint
    G /
Let's run with endurance

Bridge
Bm /   A / G / D /   Bm /   A / G /   D /
Throwing off ev'ry weight, surrounded by all God's saints
Bm /   A /   G /   D /
We shall run and not grow faint
    Gmaj7 / / / | / / / /
Let's run with endurance
    E7/G# / / / | / / / /
Let's run with endurance
    Gmaj7 / / / | / / / /
Let's run with endurance
    E7/G# / / /   G/A / / /
Let's run with endurance

Chorus (x2)
D /   A /   G / / / D /   A /   G / / /
Looking to Jesus ,   beginning and end of our faith
    D /   A /   G / / / D /   A /   G / / /   (Song end on G)
Let's run with endurance   until we behold his face

1

"Until We Behold His Face" composed by Max Horsewood
© Max Horsewood

Until We Behold His Face [Numbers]

[Default Arrangement]

Intro
1 / / **5** / / | **4** / / / | **1** / / **5** / / | **4** / / /

Verse
1 /   **5** /   **4** / / /   **1** /   **5** /   **4** / / /
In a little while, he who comes will come and will not wait
1 /   **5** /   **4** / / /   **1** /   **5** /   **4** / / /
But the righteous will live by faith, and if he shrinks back
   6ᵐ / **5** /   **4** / / /   **6ᵐ** /   **5** /   **4** / / /
My soul   has no pleasure in him
   6ᵐ / **5** /   **4** / / /   **6ᵐ** /   **5** /   **4** / / /
My soul   has no pleasure in him

Prechorus
3ᵐ /   **4** /   **5** /   **6ᵐ** /   **4** /   **1** / | **5** / / /
But we are not of those who shrink back to be destroyed
3ᵐ /   **4** /   **5** /   **6ᵐ** /   **4** /   **1** / | **5** / / /
We are the faithful ones who preserve their souls

Chorus (x2)
1 /   **5** /   **4** / / /   **1** /   **5** /   **4** / / /
Looking to Jesus ,   beginning and end of our faith
    1 /   **5** /   **4** / / /   **1** /   **5** /   **4** / / /
Let's run with endurance   until we behold his face

Bridge
6ᵐ /   **5** / **4** /   **1** /   **6ᵐ** /   **5** / **4** /   **1** /
Throwing off ev'ry weight, surrounded by all God's saints
6ᵐ /   **5** /   **4** /   **1** /
We shall run and not grow faint
    4 /
Let's run with endurance

Bridge
6ᵐ /   **5** / **4** /   **1** /   **6ᵐ** /   **5** / **4** /   **1** /
Throwing off ev'ry weight, surrounded by all God's saints
6ᵐ /   **5** /   **4** /   **1** /
We shall run and not grow faint
    4ᵐᵃʲ⁷ / / / | / / / /
Let's run with endurance
    2⁷/b5 / / / | / / / /
Let's run with endurance
    4ᵐᵃʲ⁷ / / / | / / / /
Let's run with endurance
    2⁷/b5 / / /   **4/5** / / /
Let's run with endurance

Chorus (x2)
1 /   **5** /   **4** / / /   **1** /   **5** /   **4** / / /
Looking to Jesus ,   beginning and end of our faith
    1 /   **5** /   **4** / / /   **1** /   **5** /   **4** / / /   (Song end on G)
Let's run with endurance   until we behold his face

1

"Until We Behold His Face" composed by Max Horsewood
© Max Horsewood

LISA SOLAND'S PLAYS

AN AFTERNOON WITH SHIRLEY and THE EMPTY
      CHAIR: Complementary One-Act Plays
CABO SAN LUCAS (Samuel French & Smith and Kraus)
THE CHRISTMAS TREE ANGEL RADIO DRAMA
COME TO THE GARDEN (Samuel French)
THE CORPORATE LADDER (Smith and Kraus)
DIFFERENT (Samuel French & Smith and Kraus)
DR. BISCOTTI & THE HUMAN CONDITION
      (All Original Play Publishing)
AN EARTHQUAKE (Dramatic Publishing)
THE HAND ON THE PLOUGH
HAPPY BIRTHDAY, BABY!
HOORAY FOR HOLLYWOOD (All Original Play Publishing)
IN THE UPPER ROOM (All Original Play Publishing)
INSPIRED! A Drama With Music (All Original Play
      Publishing)
THE KIND THAT DOESN'T BUDGE (Samuel French &
      Quay Magazine)
KNOTS (Samuel French & Smith and Kraus)
THE LADDER IN THE ROOM (Applause Books)
THE LADDER PLAYS
THE MAN IN THE GRAY SUIT (Samuel French)
MATT & HIS CRAZY WRITING MACHINE (All Original
      Play Publishing)
MEET CUTE
THE NAME GAME (Samuel French)
THE OTHER SHOE (Smith and Kraus)
THE ReBIRTH (Applause Books)
REBOUND AND THE BATHTUB
RED ROSES (Samuel French & Applause Books)
THE SAME THING (Samuel French & Smith and Kraus)
SERGEANT YORK: THE PLAY (All Original Play
      Publishing)
SENSITIVITY (Samuel French)
THE SNIPER'S NEST
SPATIAL DISORIENTATION (Applause Books)
THREAD COUNT (Applause Books)
TRUTH BE TOLD (Samuel French & Quay Magazine)
WAITING (Samuel French, Smith and Kraus, & Applause
Books)

What they're saying about
DR. BISCOTTI & THE HUMAN CONDITION

"Lisa Soland's *Dr. Biscotti and the Human Condition* is a tour de force and a masterpiece. Its theme centers on nothing less than life's reasons and randomness. Characters represent the fourth dimension—time rather than space. By the end of the play, we learn how life can differ for an array of people, all linked by the interlocutor—their therapist, Dr. Biscotti. This play is original, entertaining, at times shocking, and brilliantly crafted. Dramatically, it has surprises and a wonderful build to a shocking conclusion. I could not get it, or the deep philosophical and sociological issues, out of my head for weeks after seeing it. I am a long-time fan of Ms. Soland, but this is perhaps her deepest play. I would love to see it get all the attention it deserves."
– Andrew Bonime, Feature Film Producer

"Absolutely riveting dialogue and characters. *Dr. Biscotti* is an excellent work. I was absolutely captured by the characters and their stories."
– Steven L. Sears, TV Producer/Writer

What they're saying about
SERGEANT YORK: THE PLAY

"It's simply a wonderful play."
– Deborah York, Executive Director of the Sergeant York
Patriotic Foundation and great-granddaughter of Alvin York

"Sergeant York: The Play is... a powerful
statement on the nature of war
and the power of faith."
– Peter Colley, playwright/screenwriter/librettist

"I thoroughly recommend Sergeant York: The
Play for any organization seeking an
inspirational, wholesome tale of a
true American hero."
– Burt Rosen, President and CEO of Knox Area Rescue
Ministries Knoxville

"Soland has devoted her significant abilities to
share the story of Alvin York's deep personal
faith and commitment to Jesus Christ."
– Sam Polson, Lead Pastor of West Park Baptist Church

What they're saying about
30 SHORT PLAYS
FOR PASSIONATE ACTORS...

"Lisa Soland has here assembled a wonderful collection of short plays. If you're a passionate actor, a teacher or a director looking for a play to do, you won't find a better place to start looking than this book."
— *Lawrence Harbison, Senior Editor, Smith and Kraus & Applause Theatre & Cinema Books*

"Lisa Soland's amazing collection of 30 excellent, sooo entertaining short plays is a must for any would-be playwright, actor or acting group!"
— *Tom Sawyer, novelist, playwright, screenwriter*

"This collection of plays is as varied and eclectic as the human mind itself. They are funny, dramatic, poignant, shocking, outrageous, satirical, imaginative... It's a must-have for writers of short plays and a great resource for theatres that produce them."
— *Peter Colley, playwright, screenwriter, librettist*